Transform Your Self-Talk:

The Art of Talking to Yourself for Confidence, Belief, and Calm

by Nick Trenton

www.NickTrenton.com

Table of Contents

Chapter 1. That Voice Inside Your Head 6
- The Science of Self-Talk 11
- Self-Talk as an Amplifier 22
- Eenie, Meenie, Minie, Moe 27

Chapter 2. Good Versus Evil 39
- Positive Versus Negative Self-Talk 41
- A Simple Cost-Benefit Analysis 52
- Meet Your Inner Critic 60
- Five Levels of Self-Talk 69

Chapter 3. All You Need to Do Is Listen 77
- The Key to Self-Awareness 78
- Assessment Tools and Tips 91

Chapter 4. Replace, Transform, Evolve ... 107
- Three-Step Cognitive Behavioral Therapy . 109
- Step 1: Observe 111
- Step 2: Challenge 113
- Step 3: Replace 122

Chapter 5: More Than Words 143
- Everyday Reinforcement 145
- A Self-Empowerment Habit 152
- **The Culmination of Rewriting Your Self-Talk** 157

Summary Guide 169

Chapter 1. That Voice Inside Your Head

It's been there so long sometimes you barely even notice it—that little "voice" inside that quietly narrates, judges, encourages, explains or interprets the world around you. Though you may recognize the concept of an inner voice from self-help literature, the fact is there's nothing abstract or mysterious about this inner chatter. "Self-talk" actually has a surprising body of scientific evidence behind it, informing a fascinating set of theories that seek to understand exactly what's happening when we "talk to ourselves."

In this book we'll take a closer look at what self-talk actually is, the various theories that have been proposed over the years to explain the phenomenon, and the facts we've amassed so far about both its psychology and physiology.

We'll discover the different types of self-talk, investigate why it happens, explore what's normal and what's not, and most importantly, we'll see that self-talk can be changed for the better. As Bruce Lee famously said, "As you think, so shall you become." Using a series of scientifically supported techniques to identify and improve your self-talk, you can take more conscious control of your thinking and perceptions, boosting confidence, self-mastery and resilience in a challenging world.

Self-talk is something we do every day, and this is partially why it's so hard for us to change. We don't even realize we are doing it.

You wake up in the morning and the second you open your eyes the stream of thoughts starts flowing: "What day is it? Oh right, Tuesday. I mustn't forget that appointment later this afternoon. God, I have such a bad memory, why am I such an idiot all the time? I bet I'll forget it. Typical. I'm always doing things like that. Oh look, it seems like it'll be a sunny day today. That reminds me, I have to get my mole scan done at some point… but what if it's cancer? But it's not going to be. I mean, it *might* be. That would be just my luck. Great-Aunt Matilda had skin cancer. I think? If I die of cancer who will look after my kids? That would literally be the worst thing I could think of… but what's the point in getting it checked out? Doctors are all useless… That reminds me…"

You may not do all this every day, but you likely do *some* of this *some* days.

Self-talk is that stream-of-conscious, ongoing internal dialogue that runs inside our minds, affecting every aspect of our lives from our moods, to our behavior, to our self-confidence, to our appraisal of risk and reward. It's the constant conversation we have with ourselves. It can be neutral and mostly observational ("oh right, it's Tuesday"), or filled with criticism, pessimism, doom and gloom ("I shouldn't try that, I'm not good enough"). Often, all of the above become inseparable from the objective truth of a matter.

Our inner self-talk is the built-in narrator that runs alongside our lives, playing over everyday activities and in the background of every action or decision we make. This narration colors the entire tone of our lived experience, telling us how to interpret both good and bad experiences, and how to understand ourselves and our place in the world. It amounts to a narrative we tell ourselves, and this narrative is solidified well before we become adults.

Importantly, self-talk can be unconscious or conscious, negative or positive, beneficial to our lives or working entirely against our best interests. With some awareness and effort, negative and self-defeating inner talk can be identified and changed, so that the voice in your head supports rather than undermines you.

There are three primary types of self-talk.

The most obvious type is negative self-talk, and the thought-stream above is a prime example. These pessimistic interpretations, judgments, accusations, complaints, and catastrophic predictions leave us feeling awful. Some people in some circumstances might find negative self-talk motivational, but this comprises only a small percentage of negative self-talk ("They said I can't do this? I'll prove them wrong!" versus "I'm not good enough to do it, so I just won't try."). This is your inner self-critic who always sees the glass as half-empty. He can be useful and warn us about certain dangers, but again, that only takes place a rather small percentage of the time.

On the other hand, true motivational self-talk, or positive self-talk, is that which actively encourages and supports us as we navigate life's challenges, aim for our goals or cope with difficulties. This can be an affirmation-style phrase that you consciously use to correct biased thinking, or it can be simply smiling at yourself in the mirror before an interview and saying, "I'm going to be great! I can do this and I certainly deserve it!"

Neutral self-talk is the bulk of the internal conversation, and consists of simple observations and comments, while instructional self-talk is the kind of dialogue we have with ourselves to help us through certain tasks, sports or performance, for example: "keep looking straight ahead," "easy does it," and "OK, try again but this time focus on the ball..." But even these statements can take a positive or negative tone if not carefully managed.

For the purposes of our book, we'll be looking primarily at negative and positive/motivational self-talk—and how to turn the former into the latter.

The Science of Self-Talk

In 1911, neurologists Dr. Gordon Morgan Holmes and Dr. Henry Head published a series of papers exploring the connection between the body and the brain. They related a story of Victorian women who, at the time, would have worn large, fashionable feather hats and would sometimes duck to walk through a doorway even when they weren't wearing the hats.

Why? The idea is that a person's mind holds a mental picture of what their body looks like, and acts accordingly. Dr. Branch Coslett of the University of Pennsylvania found, over a century later in 2013, that women with anorexia did something similar—they angled their bodies through doorways as though to squeeze through even when they clearly had enough room. Their *mental image* of themselves didn't match their *actual* selves.

What these seemingly simple observations tell us is something rather important: that we all have a mental representation of ourselves that may or may not align with reality. We do need this internal representation (or else we'd bump into things a lot more often!), but some studies suggest that to our brains, imagining certain actions is no different neurologically to actually doing them.

It's not merely a mysterious suggestion that "thoughts create your reality;" there is a mounting body of evidence suggesting that the way you see yourself has a profound effect on your perceptions, your mental health, your behavior, and even things like your experience of pain and illness. Self-talk is the soundtrack that constantly informs us of these departures from objective reality, for better or worse.

Better stated, self-talk is one of the mechanisms we use to establish and maintain this inner representation of ourselves. Using narratives and certain kinds of language, we employ considerable brain power to literally tell ourselves who we are—and it goes way beyond giving yourself a pep talk in the mirror or saying an affirmation.

For a quick demonstration on the power of self-talk and just how specific it can be, professor Ethan Kross at the University of

Michigan published research in 2014 that showed using "I" pronouns in self-talk caused more stress and precluded feelings of self-love when compared to using your own name or "you." Have you ever spoken to yourself in the second person (e.g. "John, you've done it again!" or "You're just tired right now")? The linguistic distance created by this small shift is enough to remove you somewhat from your actions, allowing you to be kinder to yourself and give yourself more objective support.

This small change in self-talk alone seems to help people act more rationally and self-regulate more effectively. We all know how much easier it can be to be compassionate towards others than ourselves—this shift in self-talk allows us to almost treat ourselves from the outside, looking in. It's almost unfathomable for such a transformation to come from something so small, but that is indeed the basis of this book—just how damaging our normal and frequent words to ourselves are, and how much we can seize upon our potential with small changes.

For another quick demonstration of this impact, psychologist David Sarwer asks his patients with eating disorders to stand in front of a mirror and use more neutral, non-judgmental language to talk about what they see. Instead of saying "My stomach is revolting and fat, and my legs are disgusting," they practice saying "My stomach is round. My legs are pale, soft, and bigger at the top."

The idea is that you change your life not by changing your life, but by first changing *your inner representation of your life*. Just as an anorexic will never feel good about their bodies no matter what they look like, it's no use tackling external phenomenon when the problem might lie with your inner perceptions. Just as we construct mental models of what our physical body looks like so that we can interact in the world, we do the same on a psychological, emotional, relational and even spiritual levels. It turns out Bruce Lee was right—the underlying message is what's important, and not necessarily attending to the symptoms of something deeper.

Dr. Shad Helmstetter is an independent researcher who studied and observed the Amway multi-level marketing business model as an outsider for many years. He was interested in what we all secretly say to ourselves; in their case, what convinced people to join and buy into such an organization. He found that the way we talk to ourselves has profound effects on our self-perception, which in turn goes on to affect our behavior, choices, opinions, identity, relationships and more. This mechanism alone may explain why some people reach success while others seem to perpetually self-jeopardize.

Rather than believing that success is something meant for others, something that we have to be born with or even just pure luck, Dr. Helmstetter tried to show that the basic architecture of success was all in the head. The brain, he says, begins to believe whatever is repeated most often; if you consistently program yourself with self-talk that is positive and supportive, with time you create a real, physical reality that matches up with this representation of yourself. Whether it's in the area of business, relationships, family, learning, navigating life's challenges or all of these, our lives reflect the self-talk we adopt.

And actually, there is quite a bit of neuroscience to support this idea. Indeed, an entire area of brain study, including habits, muscle memory, schemas, automatic actions, and heuristics, is involved. *Neuroplasticity* is the key—i.e. the characteristic of the brain that means it can always change, physiologically and psychologically. Neuroplasticity is how any type of habit is formed. It may be helpful to think of each repetition as wearing a small groove in the brain's pathways. The more repetitions of any given thought or behavior, the deeper the groove gets, and the more ingrained it becomes within us.

This means that whatever story you're currently telling yourself, you can always stop and tell a new one. But it also means that the current story will be tough to shake.

There is a *physical* consequence to the thoughts we hold and the stories we tell—those with more negative thinking have actually been shown to have less neuronal development in certain areas of the brain than those who think positively, who develop more in the left pre-frontal cortex of the brain. This is a big deal. It means that "positive thinking" is not merely some whimsical nonsense or a comforting delusion—it's a way of actually, literally, and physically remodeling your brain to suit your own purposes.

Besides the neuroplasticity angle of self-talk, there are two additional major theories.

The first is basically that there are many discrete "I" viewpoints within one person, and that these viewpoints engage one another in internal conversation; i.e., self-talk is essentially an inner dialogue between different parts of yourself. This is called the Dialogical Self Theory (DST). The other theory suggests that ordinary language and inner self-talk are basically the same thing, and are both relational. There is a two-way relationship between words and their meanings, and this relationship comes from within us and from the society we live in. This is called the Relational Frame Theory (RFT).

The Dialogical Self Theory

The "I" in self-talk can be many different people—a child, a parent, a worker, a partner, an adversary, etc. Each of these identities has different feelings, desires, needs, and fears, and sometimes they conflict with one another. The "I" that is a diligent employee may conflict with the "I" that is a loving parent (for example, missing time with your child because you often work overtime at a job you also love), and the resulting inner dialogue is one that can help us resolve the tension or else keep us feeling trapped and unhappy.

Have you ever heard a judgmental inner voice only to realize it's not really your own, but the voice of an internalized parent, boss or partner? This happens because the perspectives of others can become part of our own dialogical selves. Dialogical Self Theory may be a useful theory to work with if you frequently find your self-talk arguing against itself, or you often feel guilty, unsure of who you are, conflicted, and so on. By asking how your various perspectives interact with each other, you can begin to find cooperation between them.

The Relational Frame Theory (RFT)

Language, self-talk and emotion are all constantly engaging with one another. Self-talk and language in general share one interesting characteristic in common: they are relational. This means that we respond to a stimulus in terms of another stimulus: things are like or unlike other things, or they relate to them in hierarchical, special or comparative terms. In other words, language constantly refers back to itself.

Self-talk is also relational in this way, and all the symbols it uses are interconnected to one another every time we ruminate, overthink, self-criticize or indeed self-praise. The benefits of language largely depend on *how* we use it. We can use language to dream up all sorts of novel and even impossible concepts, but we are always deeply affected by the language we use. It follows then that we should be aware of and willing to rework the relational frames we employ in our self-talk.

Both theories are attractive and go a long way to explaining the phenomena that modern cognitive psychology research is investigating to this day. For our purposes, however, the most important takeaway is that self-talk is not a fixed fact of life, but can be changed no matter the mechanism through which it presents. These theories are focused on the "why," and we are focused on the "how to change and improve" in this book.

Self-Talk as an Amplifier

Talking aloud to oneself conjures up certain images—perhaps a mad scientist furiously muttering to himself as he works. You've probably heard the old wives' tale that "talking to yourself" means you're crazy, and many people are reluctant to admit it or feel embarrassed if caught talking aloud to themselves. Do you loudly chastise yourself for making a mistake, give yourself a little pep talk in the bathroom mirror before a first date, or mentally say things like, "Okay, think carefully, where did you leave it? Don't panic!"?

Rest assured this is all perfectly normal. When you think about it, isn't this exactly what *thinking* is? Most of us are engaged in an almost nonstop stream of self-talk and talk to ourselves so often that we've actually become unaware of ourselves doing it. Inner talk is one thing, but people can worry that talking *out loud* to themselves is somehow different, and spells trouble.

Actually, it's a habit that is astoundingly common, and can even help us process things better. For example, speaking thoughts aloud slows them down and heightens focused awareness. By activating our language centers, we concretize and formalize our thoughts into something we can work with more tangibly—and this often has the effect of calming us down. Self-talk has the capacity to amplify whatever you want, but it comes down to whether you can harness this power.

Talking to yourself engages your meta-cognition and higher order processing, and gives you a chance to process emotions. In fact, grasping the fundamentals of language and self-talk may be the very thing that helps us develop self-control as children, according to developmental psychologist Jean Piaget.

An interesting 2001 study by Gruber and Cramon found that monkeys use different parts of their brain to do a visual matching task than they do an auditory matching task, but humans actually use both areas of the brain for both activities. However, the study also showed that humans can behave more like monkeys in this respect if they prevent self-talk, for example by saying mindless words like "blah blah blah" during the task. This study shows that self-talk has direct effects on our self-control of our behavior—or rather, it has the potential to aid us in broad and fundamental ways.

A study by Alexander Kirkham at Bangor University showed that talking out loud enhances self-control when doing a task, more so than merely saying things quietly in your own mind. Concentration skills and overall performance were improved in those who spoke aloud as they completed a task. So, the next time you talk aloud to yourself, be grateful for the hard work your brain might be doing for you!

Occupational therapist Dr. Julia Harper explains, however, that just because self-talk is common and normal, that doesn't necessarily mean it's always *beneficial*. The way we talk to ourselves makes all the difference. It may seem fairly obvious, but the "good" kind of self-talk is all about neutral and helpful statements, using positive and supportive language, which frames things in a way that is more likely to inspire your success. In other words, the content and emotional tone of what you say matters most.

Random and distracting thoughts running in every direction, mindless mental chatter, and an inability to focus on relevant information can in fact be bad for our mental health. An out-of-control, wandering mind may have us unconsciously linking ideas and making nonsensical associations that can lead to inappropriate responses or incoherence. But note that it's not self-talk per se that is the problem, but whether we are able to use self-talk properly and appropriately to serve our goals.

When used with discernment, self-talk has plenty of benefits. A 2012 study in the *Quarterly Journal of Experimental Psychology* by Lupyan and Swingley showed that people more quickly found lost objects when they repeated out loud the name of the object to themselves as they searched. Neuroscientist Dr. Don Vaughn also explains that talking out loud while studying boosts retention, and self-talk can act as a kind of "spoken journal" to help you work through difficult emotions. Self-talk is a way for the brain to organize its thoughts, solidify memories, regulate emotions and plan future behavior. Talking aloud is no different from silent self-talk, but merely an extension of it.

Ultimately, self-talk is something that is not only normal, but potentially very useful, if done consciously. We'll discuss becoming more aware of and mindful of inner talk later in the book, but for now, whenever you talk to yourself, commit to actually listening as well! Pause and take a moment to process. Ask yourself questions and give yourself support or encouragement.

Talking out loud to yourself is not a sign of mental illness, but could actually be evidence of high cognitive function, memory, and conscious control of your intellectual faculties. That being said, anxious and uncontrollable mental chatter that runs away with itself is not likely to have the same effect.

If you're up in the early hours of the morning ruminating and getting carried away with anxious thoughts, you may find that assigning your brain a task like reading could stop unhealthy self-talk and get you relaxed again. Likewise, self-talk, aloud or silent, is not a problem when directed to yourself, but may be a cause for concern if addressed to hallucinations or people who aren't really there.

Eenie, Meenie, Minie, Moe

As we've seen in the previous section, not all self-talk is created equal. There are many variations, and some types are more helpful than others. If you've been wondering exactly what counts as self-talk, consider that all of the following can be considered self-talk:

- Making positive or negative statements to yourself ("This will fail" or "You got this!")
- Conscious or unconscious silent inner speech that may follow a dialogue ("You can't have left the keys at the store because you had them when you arrived home. But what if you left the door unlocked and just came in? Well, I never leave the door unlocked, I must have had my keys with me...")
- Out loud self-talk (Saying "you idiot!" when you make a mistake, or rehearsing your shopping list to yourself in the car)
- Out of control and anxious rumination, such as the racing thoughts that come with depression or panic attacks.

Research into the different kinds of self-talk has led to diverse findings in all kinds of areas, including education, sports psychology, neural development and even personality. As we saw earlier, the quality of one's self-talk can have either positive or negative effects, but some of the more recent research has found that self-talk:

- Helps with emotional regulation (such as in the research conducted by Mischel et al., 1996 and Carver and Scheier, 1998).
- Helps with self-distancing if using "you" statements or your own name rather than "I" pronouns (as we saw with Kross in a previous section). This gives you the room to take a more neutral and compassionate perspective on yourself.
- Helps you give self-instruction and self-motivation (see Hatzigeorgiadis et al., 2011). This is common in sports where coaches recommend verbally saying aloud, "You're doing great! Just take it easy, that's it…"
- Improves your sense of self-awareness, bolstering a more accurate self-evaluation and encouraging more mindful reflection on how your brain is working, and how that in turn affects both your emotions and your behavior (see research done by White et al., 2015 and Morin, 2018).

- Strengthens and fortifies certain cognitive processes (Langland-Hassan and Vicente, 2018), including perspective-taking and monitoring language development and speech production.
- Helps with regulating the emotions and coping with painful or difficult experiences (Orvell et al., 2019 and Kross et al., 2014, 2017), encouraging mental toughness and emotional resilience.

If that seems like a lot of benefits, then you're beginning to understand why this area of research has garnered so much attention!

Some researchers have used the STS, or Self-Talk Scale, to identify four main types of self-talk. These include self-criticism after negative events, self-praise and reinforcement after positive events, self-management and the attempt to decide what to do and how, and social-assessment, which is self-talk that refers to social interactions in the past, present or future.

Each of these four types likely overlaps, with a mix of different effects and functions which heavily depend on the context, the person doing the self-talk and its intensity and duration.

Though different theorists, coaches and thinkers will refer to slightly different definitions and models of self-talk, the key point to bear in mind is that self-talk varies greatly. It can be helpful or unhelpful, conscious or unconscious, cruel or compassionate, sensible or deranged, inspiring or completely self-sabotaging.

Our goal with this book is to use some of these theories as a springboard to gain a better understanding of our own self-talk. This can be done with conscious awareness, calm compassion, and a little curiosity. You might notice that you have a running narrative going on in your head whenever you speak to others, or that you sometimes adopt a very harsh and overly critical attitude to yourself when you believe you've failed. For instance, a small selection of the types of negative self-talk we might want to become aware of and avoid:

- Overreaction: "Everything is terrible."
- Personalization: "Why is this happening to me?", "It's my fault."
- Absolute language: "I'm a bad person."
- Assumption: "He thinks I'm not good enough!"
- Expectation: "This isn't how it's supposed to be!"
- Comparison: "Why can't I be like her?"
- Regret: "If I hadn't done that..."

Self-talk can be a one-off statement or a deeply held core belief that you return to again and again, not being even slightly aware of the alternatives. People battling depression or low self-esteem may have a relentless repeat of the same self-talk playing in their mind 24/7. Others may end up putting a lot of their self-talk down on ink and paper, or find that their "inner critic" is actually the voice of someone else they've taken on as their own.

Whatever your self-talk is, you can consciously pause and watch it happen, and decide deliberately whether the stories you tell truly align with the goals you want to reach in life. Every time you talk to yourself, you are potentially cementing limiting and harmful habits and keeping yourself in a place you don't want to be.

On the other hand, according to Dr. Helmstetter, we can choose to engage in the more beneficial and affirming forms of self-talk:

- *Habit-changing self-talk* is that which deliberately seeks to break away from old habits rather than strengthen them. For example, pausing every time you think "I'm stupid" to consciously change your wording to "I'm learning." This self-talk is establishing a new habit—one of self-esteem and kindness.
- *Attitude-changing self-talk* aims to build up your positive self-belief and esteem, for example, "I'm trying my best and I'm doing great."
- *Motivational self-talk* goes a step further and takes the form of affirmations and self-encouragement as we attempt something scary or new.

- *Situational self-talk* is about taking a different perspective on situations in life, such as changing frameworks to deal with adversity, accidents or problems as they arise. For example, "How am I going to smooth things over here?" or "How can I look at this problem differently?"

In this chapter, we've looked at what self-talk is, the different types, and how it can help or harm, as well as some common theories used to understand the phenomenon. And you're hopefully convinced that there is nothing strange about occasionally muttering to yourself under your breath!

In the following chapters, we'll further flesh out some of these concepts, so you feel able to not only understand your own inner talk, but gain conscious mastery over it. You might naturally be wondering how to start changing your negative self-talk into a more positive internal dialogue. But to do that, we first need to fully understand the difference.

Takeaways

- Have you ever noticed a voice inside your head that is constantly chattering about something or the other right from the moment you wake up? You might have grown so accustomed to it that you barely notice it anymore, but it's definitely there, and it's either hurting or helping you. No perspective is truly neutral. This voice, a part of your stream of consciousness, is an inner monologue that runs alongside your life, observing and commenting on its various happenings. It tells you who you are, and how you should feel about your identity and the events that occur in your life.
- There are three main types of inner voices or self-talk. The first is positive self-talk, which acts as a continuous reaffirmation of the good things about you and your life. This type of inner voice bolsters our confidence and elevates happiness levels. However, on the other end lies negative self-talk. This voice is always critical and saying degrading

things to us about who we are, what we do, etc. If left uncontrolled, it can lead to several mental health issues. The third type is neutral self-talk, which simply consists of unbiased observations as we walk through life—although this almost always has a positive or negative subtext.

- Our inner voice, regardless of type, represents the inner representation we have of ourselves. Often, this is not consistent with reality. The way we think we are and what we actually are can be miles apart, but reality seldom matters if we're convinced that things are a certain way. This leads to why having healthy self-talk is so important. It influences our thoughts, perceptions, and the way we view ourselves, all of which have physiological correlations that affect how we feel and behave. The basis behind this is neuroplasticity, as the more you repeat something, the more it changes your brain's structure and becomes your reality.

- If you're wondering what exactly counts as self-talk, it includes positive or negative statements we say to ourselves, our ruminations, racing thoughts, and the conversations we have with ourselves. Regulating this self-talk can have many positive effects that are essential to our well-being, such as improving sports performances, reducing stress, promoting better self-esteem, and helping us cope with the ups and downs of life. Monitoring self-talk is the key to changing your emotions, behavior, perspective, and life potential.

Chapter 2. Good Versus Evil

Positive self-talk is everything that helps us regulate our emotions, work through memories or complicated experiences, maintain awareness of ourselves and our world, and encourage ourselves as we deal with problems or challenging situations. It is the set of messages we constantly repeat in our heads over and over that help us see the optimism, joy, and hope in any given situation. This is the angel perched on our left shoulder, while the right shoulder has, well, the devil.

Positive self-talk *sounds* simple, but the fact is that so many people consistently engage in negative self-talk despite desperately wanting to do better. We end up internalizing negative and irrational messages about who we are, the way we act, our abilities, etc., from external sources. Recognizing self-talk as it's happening is simple but not easy—because we are so used to our constant internal chatter, we may forget we're even doing it. Heck, you are doing it right now when reading through a process called *subvocalization*.

Rather than being aware of the fact that we are running a constant internal narration, we assume that we are simply perceiving life as it is, i.e. that the story we are telling ourselves is true, objective fact. This is especially the case when our self-talk coincides with our fears or implicit beliefs about who we really are. However, with some attention and effort, we can use our self-talk to reaffirm positivity in a way that keeps anxiety and negativity at bay while allowing us to accomplish goals that we previously considered beyond our capabilities.

Positive Versus Negative Self-Talk

Positive self-talk doesn't mean you indulge in over-the-top and insincere self-flattery, and it isn't vain or unrealistic. Brazenly telling yourself, "It's going to happen this time, I just know it" as you buy a lottery ticket might be considered by some to be positive thinking, but it's not a particularly helpful line of thinking, not least because it won't change your chances of winning!

When people engage in cognitive behavioral therapy (more on this in a later chapter) they are essentially attempting to undo negative self-talk, and replace it not with flowery platitudes but with more neutral, rational statements that more closely align with reality. We are our own worst critics, and that can often lead us to ignore genuine positives in a way that becomes detrimental to our mental well-being.

Though most people struggle with overly negative rather than overly positive thinking, what you really want is to aim for thinking that a) most closely lines up with the real world around you and b) actually helps you achieve the goals that are important to you.

So, when we talk about "positive" self-talk, we can also imagine it means balanced, self-aware, healthy, and useful self-talk. We want to avoid distorting reality or behaving in ways that undermine our goals—whether that's in overly positive or overly negative ways. If the reality is negative, we want to find a way to accept and feel better about it, and if it's positive, we want to believe in it and have confidence.

We now know there is no value in endlessly bolstering self-esteem with excessive praise. Far healthier is a balanced, robust perspective that has a respectful relationship with reality, including its dark sides!

Consider the following self-talk phrases:

Thought A: "I'm a hideous fat blob and I'm ugly. I can't bear for anyone to look at me."

Thought B: "I'm beautiful and perfect in every way!"

Thought C: "I'm OK with how I look. I could probably lose a few pounds, but I have some attractive features too and besides, there's so much more to me than how I look."

Thought D: "Your BMI is slightly into the overweight category, but only by a few pounds, and your overall health is excellent."

Which of these thoughts is the "right" one? Which is positive and which negative? You'll notice that the actual appearance of this person is beside the point. Which thought is more likely to lead to a resilient sense of self-esteem, well-being and beneficial actions toward meaningful goals?

Thought A is negative, overly emotional and likely to lead to apathy and self-hate (whether it's "true" or not!), whereas Thought B is "positive" but not in the least likely to encourage honest self-appraisal of areas that need improvement. Thoughts C and D are more neutral, though D is mostly negative until the very end, by which time you're more likely to focus on the bad than what is good. It's Thought C that strikes a balance between "true" and compassionate.

It recognizes room for improvement ("I could lose a few pounds"), but stays positive overall.

This is what we mean by positive self-talk. Rumination (i.e. endlessly turning over worst-case scenarios in your head, all-or-nothing statements, overly emotional judgments, criticisms, anxious overthinking and "what if?" thoughts than you can't seem to switch off...) is neither objective nor encouraging. This, along with statements that criticize or undermine, is what we mean by negative self-talk. And the subsequent impact it has on self-image, perspective, and self-worth is significant.

So, generating positive self-talk doesn't merely involve turning a negative self-talk statement into its equally unrealistic opposite. Real self-esteem doesn't rely on falsely boosting the ego—this exaggeration is only more of the same and will never feel truly satisfying. Rather, it's the calm and stable awareness that comes with knowing *you* are in control of your mind, you can be aware of and respectful of your feelings, and you have irreducible value and worth as a human being, no matter what.

In many ways, trying to convert negative to positive can come with perils—we risk reinforcing limiting perspectives and further digging ourselves into a hole. For example, if a person struggled with their weight (as in the above examples) they might decide to substitute more positive self-talk that claimed, "You are overweight and some people like that more, which makes you superior to other skinny and malnourished-looking people, and proves that you're kinder and more intelligent than those other superficial people…"

It's not positive thinking to be baselessly proud of legitimate flaws and mistakes, to compare yourself to others, or to put others down. You also might have noticed that "everyone hates me" and "everyone loves me" share the same weakness—they put the locus of worth *outside* of the person, rather than inside, making for a self-esteem that is fragile and inauthentic.

Let's look at some other examples.

Negative:

This is too hard and I can't do it.

Success should come quickly and with no effort.

Positive:

I'm proud of how hard I've worked. I don't have to be the best in the world, but I really tried, and I learnt a lot in the process.

Negative:

Nobody is interested in dating a loser like me.

Women are so shallow these days.

Positive:

Dating can be tough sometimes, but I'm using the opportunity to learn about myself and grow where I can.

Negative:

There's no hope of changing things so I may as well give up now.

Life is unfair, what's new?

Positive:

I can't tell what the future holds, but I know I will always do my best to live according to my own principles.

A lot of your inner talk may appear to be rather neutral—i.e. when you're instructing yourself on how to do something or making an observation about the environment. But the self-talk we're interested in is all those statements that seem to address us directly, and go toward building that inner representation of ourselves and how we relate to the external world.

It can be difficult to give examples of good and bad self-talk because self-talk is always going to be unique to every person and their context. There are some general sentiments and attitudes, however, that lead to self-talk statements that most of us can probably find useful in our lives.

If you're unsure about what constitutes positive self-talk, you may consider the following positive statements and try them on for size in your own life. If they feel overly foreign, outlandishly positive, or even unthinkable, it's probably pretty clear that you aren't used to thinking of yourself in a positive manner.

At this early stage, it might be useful to notice which statements you feel most resistant to, or which seem most at odds with your own worldview.

- This isn't what I wanted to happen, but I've definitely learnt some valuable lessons.
- This is just a thought, and a thought can change.
- I can always choose how I respond to adversity.
- I can always choose what stories I tell about myself.
- Though this is challenging, I can always keep trying, and every challenge is an opportunity to learn something new.

- I don't have to do everything perfectly all the time.
- I accept that I sometimes feel down and unhappy, because I accept myself.
- I am proud of all that I have achieved and overcome so far.
- I'm a person worthy of respect and compassion and I have value, no matter what.
- I will try hard not to worry about things I can't control.
- My opinion, my boundaries, my goals and my preferences all matter.
- No matter where I am now, I can learn, grow and change.
- There may be some things I can't do, but I can try, experiment and adapt.

You may notice something about the above sentiments: they are all *internal*, and can be held no matter what external circumstances you find yourself in, good or bad. The truth is that the world can be difficult and confusing at times, and we don't have endless control over everything that happens to us.

But we do have control over what we consciously create in our own minds, and we can always choose the story that best allows us to feel good and achieve what's important to us. No matter what form it takes, positive self-talk reinforces the belief that on a fundamental level, "I am enough."

Negative self-talk, on the other hand, only undermines your goals, potential, talents, value and abilities. These are the thoughts that lead to inaction and apathy, to hiding away from life, to depression and anxiety, fragile thinking, giving up, blaming others or avoidance. Negative self-talk is perhaps even more varied and unique to the person thinking it, but it, too, has some common elements that you'll see cropping up again and again:

- I'm not worth making the effort for, I'm not worth compassion or understanding, I'm not worth fighting for or protecting, I'm not worth any investment of time or energy.

- I can't do this, or anything. I'm useless/stupid and I'm not capable of improving.
- I could try and make an effort, but there's no real point, because nothing I do makes any difference anyway.
- I'll be rejected if I try, people will laugh at me and judge me, and people don't like me as I am.
- Other people are smarter, better looking, more successful, kinder and just better than I am. When compared to others, I'm inferior.
- I won't bother hoping for anything or starting something new because I know I won't finish it, and I don't have a hope of achieving my goals.
- I'm a failure. I have to be perfect or I shouldn't even bother. I can't make any mistakes or I'm a bad person.
- What I think doesn't matter in the grand scheme of things.
- I can't really trust life or myself.
- People are bad and always will be.

- I have to compete with everyone around me and there is never enough to go around.

Phew! It's easy to see how negative self-talk is a one-way ticket to depression and low self-esteem. Let's hope that you didn't find those sentiments too familiar or frequent in your life. Underneath many of these different thoughts and feelings is one core belief: "I am not enough."

Much of our negative self-talk stems from a fundamental disbelief in our own value. We believe that we are fundamentally useless, and need to prove to others how good we are in order to be considered worthy. We take failure personally, criticize ourselves harshly and self-sabotage everything good or promising in our lives because deep down, it doesn't fit with the story we've spent so much time telling ourselves: "I am not enough."

A Simple Cost-Benefit Analysis

Motivational speaker Tony Robbins has said, "Change happens when the pain of staying the same is greater than the pain of change." When we truly understand the cost of engaging in negative self-talk and compare it to the potential gains of adopting positive self-talk, the choice to change is an obvious one.

Benefits of positive self-talk

So far, we've been considering the most obvious benefit of positive self-talk: it makes us feel good. Supportive, compassionate, and encouraging self-talk understandably strengthens self-esteem. Though we often seek validation from others, positive self-talk allows us to motivate ourselves. But there are more benefits, the main one being a reduction of stress levels.

A 2004 research paper by Iwanaga, Yokoyama and Seiwa suggests that those with more positive self-talk habits typically have better coping mechanisms when faced with stressful life scenarios or challenges. It makes sense. If you can gently re-frame a problem, you give yourself a fresh perspective that allows you to see new solutions and opportunities, while reducing the stress of feeling disempowered.

A 2008 study by Lyubormisky found that optimistic people with healthy self-esteem simply do better in life, whether it's performance at school, recovery from injury or achieving general life goals. In other words, positive thinking is a self-fulfilling prophesy. When you believe and behave as if you are fit for the task of life, you are more likely to approach events with exactly the attitude most conducive to success.

In a 2012 paper titled *Optimism: An enduring resource for romantic relationships* by Assad, Donnellan, and Conger, the researchers discovered that couples who were optimistic cooperated more and had generally better relationship outcomes. This also makes sense: people who are confident, proactive, and compassionate are always going to make better partners!

Positive self-talk has been associated with a wide range of outcomes including better performance in sport, healing body dysmorphia and eating disorders, and more effective education. Most importantly, healthy self-talk can alleviate mental health issues like depression, PTSD, stress, anxiety, poor self-esteem, and aggression (see Leung and Poon, 2000; Owens and Chard, 2001; Kendall and Treadwell, 2007).

The benefits of positive self-talk are so wide-ranging because the neurotransmitters associated with such thoughts (for example serotonin, dopamine and GABA) affect every part of the body. This is another aspect of neuroplasticity we reserved for this chapter. Most of us think of emotions as abstract, airy things, but they have a *physiological reality* in our bodies, regulating our feelings of well-being, motivation, energy levels, interest in life and ability to relax and feel good about ourselves.

The system goes both ways: neurotransmitters affect how we think and feel, but thoughts and feelings in turn can affect neurotransmitter levels—which then go on to have an effect on every bodily system. Thoughts are first converted into electrochemical signals in the brain, which is then stimulated to release hormones and neurotransmitters that travel throughout the body, affecting the structure and function of every tissue and organ.

How Negative Self-Talk Sabotages Your Life

Positive self-talk can leave you feeling calmer, more proactive, and more confident about your life, but the flipside is that negative self-talk does exactly the opposite. It's easy to imagine that being talked down to and insulted throughout the day (which is exactly what negative self-talk is!) would leave you feeling bad emotionally. It turns out there are real, neurological reasons why.

When you engage in negative self-talk, you encourage your body to release chemicals called catecholamines from your adrenal glands, for example dopamine and norepinephrine. Your body responds to the "threat" of this self-talk as though it were any other danger, even producing cortisol that permeates through the entire body.

Cortisol has lasting effects on the body. It compromises the immune system and decreases the volume of the left pre-frontal cortex—the part of your brain associated with positive emotions. Thinking about yourself negatively affects your body, not just your feelings. Even worse, a self-fulfilling feedback loop is established, wherein the more negatively we think, the easier it is to keep on thinking negatively, and so on. The basic upshot is that you are in a constant state of stress and alarm, and each thought will build upon the previous one. It's only a matter of time until you explode like Mount Vesuvius.

The stress that comes with negative self-talk affects every single part of the body. You may tell yourself "I'm a failure" and then feel stressed and anxious. This causes a physiological response throughout your nervous system, which in chronic cases can affect your brain, leading you to keep thinking negatively… It's a vicious cycle.

Most of us tend to think of negative self-talk, low confidence and so on as merely emotional or psychological phenomena, and not something "real" like cancer or a broken leg. But nothing could be further from the truth. Negative self-talk actively undermines your physical health. This is because you *are* your body. Your body and brain (and all the thoughts in it) are not two different things!

You may notice unexplained gastrointestinal trouble like a stomach in knots, bloating or discomfort. Ulcers are most commonly associated with stress. Heart attacks, of course, happen to young and healthy people because they are in so much distress.

You also may feel completely exhausted and wiped out for seemingly no reason. Constant negative self-talk can wear you down over time, leaving your motivation for life at a low ebb. Some people find that negative self-talk impacts sleep (all that three a.m. catastrophizing!), and all this combined can certainly make it harder to focus and concentrate.

Negative self-talk leaves us feeling pessimistic, hopeless, irritable, and apathetic—and it's all due to our system being chronically bathed in stress hormones. Negative self-talk is associated with many of the symptoms we think of as accompanying generally poor mental health: changes in appetite, getting sick often, random aches and pains, and low mood. This is all without mentioning just how disempowered you might feel when bombarded with constant negative self-talk, and how you might never reach your dreams or goals because, well, you've told yourself they're "*impossible.*"

And it all starts with something decidedly *nonphysical*: your thoughts. Unfortunately, we all suffer from something called the negativity bias. This bias refers to the phenomenon wherein we tend to focus on and emphasize negative stimuli far more than we do positive stimuli. This is because our brains require more neural processing to interpret negative stimuli, causing it to have a longer-lasting effect on both our minds and bodies. Though the bias has its roots in the evolutionary advantages it provided—avoiding negative experiences protected our ancestors from danger—it can make negative thoughts that much more challenging to cope with. In a way, we're hard-wired to be negative, and it is this very impulse that we need to learn to overcome.

None of us would fare very well if we had a team of "reverse cheerleaders" following us around all day, yelling insults, criticizing our every move, and telling us how awful we looked every time we walked past a mirror. And yet, many of us *are* experiencing this very reality every day, only it is self-inflicted and invisible.

Meet Your Inner Critic

If positive self-talk is so great and negative self-talk so harmful, why do so many of us engage in negative self-talk?

What's the source of this devastating little voice inside?

Some people have called it the "inner critic," and it's that internal voice which criticizes, demeans, belittles or judges us, often with little respect for what is actually true. This voice shapes our identity, sense of worth and our belief in what's possible. You'll know the inner critic is speaking when its weapon of choice against you seems to be shame, guilt or fear.

It can be enlightening to think about where and why we first acquired this inner narrative voice. It's certainly not a choice. Your life experiences, the way you've been parented, social expectations, cultural norms and all the details of your unique context may set up this voice inside you.

The inner critic itself has been theorized to come from the internalized voices of others who at some point really did criticize or undermine you. If you are frequently told "you're useless," it's no surprise that you would soon come to tell yourself the same thing, long after the words were first uttered. If you grow up in a culture or family environment that stresses competition, a scarcity mindset, or shame, then you may live as though this is a normal way to think and feel.

For those with chronic self-doubt, low self-worth or even beliefs that border on the delusional (such as a beauty pageant winner insisting she's hideous, or the woman with "imposter syndrome" who believes she has achieved nothing even though she's a successful CEO), it can be helpful to ask about the origin of this voice.

Is the little voice really *yours*? Many people are surprised to notice that their inner critic sounds suspiciously like their parents, previous teachers, or other critical voices.

Just as negative self-talk can cause depression, it can also be a symptom of depression and other mood disorders. Being highly self-critical can accompany a host of health conditions, mental and physical. But in a way, it doesn't matter all that much *why* you think as you do, only that you do. It can be incredibly healing to see that your inner voice doesn't even strictly belong to you. This voice is a combination of your conscious and subconscious thoughts, along with the host of external influences that we encounter in our daily lives.

If you see that your self-talk is not based in reality and is actively causing you harm while shutting out many good things in life, you can work toward making changes, no matter the cause or source of your self-talk.

If your self-talk is a little engine or machine that churns to produce statements, beliefs and feelings, then self-esteem is the fuel that it runs on.

Your brain is a powerful tool, but it can only process what it's given: feed it with low-esteem (i.e., fuel it with the fundamental belief that "I am not enough") and all its output will be negative and self-denying. Feed it with healthy self-esteem (i.e., fuel it with the fundamental belief that "I am enough") and its output will be life-affirming, goal oriented, and optimistic.

Your beliefs inform your thinking, which then cements those original beliefs and inspires your behavior, which then produces results that feed back into your original beliefs. And so the cycle continues, and soon you believe "this is how I am" when in fact all you have been doing is telling yourself a very convincing story for a very long time.

But what is this fuel for optimism, self-esteem? We've alluded to it in earlier sections, mentioning how self-esteem is *not* idealistic optimism, vanity, narcissism, denial of the facts of life or wishful thinking.

Self-esteem is essentially our own self-concept, or the sense of who we are in the world. It's all about how we perceive ourselves, and how we feel about who we think we are. Positive and strong self-esteem means we experience ourselves as good, worthy and lovable people whom others view in good terms. Negative or weak self-esteem has us feeling like people who are unloved, wrong, broken, stupid, unworthy or just *bad*.

Our self-esteem comes from many sources—past experiences, our own personal development, our goals and expectations, our relationships to others, our culture, family history, gender, belief system, age and more. It can be stable or change with time, and takes dips and boosts with life's seasons.

We all have the ability to feel as though we are largely satisfied with ourselves, flaws and all. Having good self-esteem comes down to believing that you have innate worth and many good qualities. It's "having a good reputation with yourself" and generally liking and respecting yourself, with a moderate expectation that others may do the same.

If we dig a little, we see that negative self-talk is actually just a symptom of our inner beliefs about ourselves, i.e. our self-esteem. But that begs the question: what causes low self-esteem?

There's plenty of evidence to suggest that our experiences with our primary caregivers as children shapes our perception of our self-worth and consequently, determines the tone and content of much of our self-talk. We may develop low self-esteem because of:

- Disapproving/critical authority figures who caused feelings of shame ("you'll never amount to anything").
- Caregivers who were neglectful or too preoccupied with their own lives to pay you attention when you most needed to be acknowledged and praised. This can leave you feeling unimportant, invisible, unknown, and not worth noticing.

- Caregivers who fought with each other. Young children can internalize the feeling that they are to blame.
- Bullying at home or school, and feeling as though you weren't important enough to be protected. Can create feelings of being abandoned, lost, or victimized.
- Overly coddling or supportive parents. They may have made you feel like their support was unwarranted and exaggerated, causing deep shame about who you "really" are.
- Receiving no support through academic challenges, making you feel stupid or defective.
- Sexual, physical, or emotional abuse can make a child believe their will is not worth as much as others', that they are worthless, or even to blame for what happened to them.
- Cultural or religious beliefs that emphasize shame and judgement for who you are—this can include unrealistic images and ideology from the media.
- Low confidence may even have a genetic component; we may each be born with

different levels of serotonin and oxytocin (hormones associated with happiness and well-being) and this affects our temperament, which in turn affects our behavior. Some people have personalities that are more cautious, watchful or inhibited, which is not necessarily a bad thing, but may preclude high confidence.
- Life experiences can prime us for poor self-esteem, for example harassment, trauma, or discrimination.
- Low self-esteem can, as we saw above, also be a side effect of other mental health issues such as anxiety and depression.
- Certain childhood traumas can have us internalizing the blame for things that aren't our fault, and converting it into a deep feeling of shame that we carry into adulthood.

Not everyone who experiences the above will develop poor self-esteem, and not everyone with poor self-esteem has necessarily experienced these things. Most importantly, though understanding childhood causes of low self-esteem can be insightful, it doesn't mean we are bound to our past. We can always change. Understanding why we feel as we do, we can start taking steps to build a healthier, more realistic internal picture of who we are.

The parenting you received is not the only possible source of low self-worth. Many of us engage in daily habits that actively erode our self-esteem and lead to negative self-talk, without us even realizing it.

It seems obvious, but not taking care of yourself physically makes it so much harder to care for yourself mentally. Poor health habits can be damaging in many ways—denying and neglecting our own care sends a message that we are not worth more.

Similarly, spending too much time alone can lead to rumination that isn't balanced by the input of socializing or other activities. Several studies have found that prolonged isolation increases stress, which acts as a gateway to depression and anxiety, thereby reducing self-esteem. Being socially isolated can also lead to us hesitating to ask for help we really need it, closing ourselves off to sources of affirmation and support in the process. We neglect our own self-care and barely notice that we're "running on empty."

Finally, spending too much time around overly negative people can also invite negative self-talk, especially if those people are critical, judgmental, or cruel to you. Deliberately avoiding discussing or fixing relationship problems is a common but underrated sign of lack of self-care, and only maintains poor self-image and negative self-talk.

Five Levels of Self-Talk

As you can see, self-talk is something that both establishes and maintains our faulty narratives about ourselves. But when we deliberately choose our own self-talk, we can change the process, and use our self-talk to create ourselves in a new image—one that *we* choose.

The process of improving self-talk usually happens by degree—we don't become healthy and balanced overnight. As we slowly gain healthier self-esteem, we are able to generate self-talk of an increasingly higher quality.

Level 1 self-talk is harmful self-talk that reinforces a negative narrative about ourselves. Becoming aware of this kind of inner dialogue and why it's present has been the focus of the book so far. This is the most common level of self-talk, so don't fret if you find yourself at level 1 right now. Most people, unfortunately, may never move past this level. Some relevant examples are:

"I can't do this."

"I wish life were fair but it's not."

"I suck."

Level 2 self-talk is a slight improvement in that it recognizes a need for changes to be made, even though it doesn't offer any actual solutions.

"I really should exercise more."

"I've got to do something about my low mood."

"This can't go on anymore."

Level 3 self-talk takes things a step further into actual practice. However, if we don't act on our thoughts from level 2, it leads us to regress back to level 1. In level 3, we use our self-talk to our desired ends, deciding to help ourselves by actively reprogramming a new image of ourselves. Notice these examples are framed in present tense, which means they are somewhat subject to change and not wholly certain:

"I find things to be grateful for every day."

"I'm calm and focused right now."

"I won't crave unhealthy food."

Level 4 self-talk goes in and replaces all level 1 and 2 self-talk, working comprehensively to shape our new identities with self-respect, self-belief and positivity. This is a level of belief that is not false or forced.

"I'm a positive person."

"I act with resilience and awareness."

Level 5 self-talk is about a more universal affirmation and acceptance of ourselves and everyone else. In fact, it even becomes negative in the sense that it acknowledges negativity and accepts it. This is the broadest view possible, and a wholesale affirmation of life itself.

"I focus on the things I can control."

"I choose my thoughts, my values and my actions."

"I may be overweight but I am content with this."

Glancing at these different levels or kinds of self-talk, you may ask yourself where the bulk of your mental effort and energy goes. Is it into negative statements that don't go anywhere, only make you feel bad? Do you frequently note a problem but never take steps to move on from it? Most of us work on levels 1 and 2 only. However, once we proceed to level 3, the path ahead becomes much simpler because we start reaping the benefits of our healthy practices. As we proceed to level 4, and finally level 5, we start to exercise decisive control over the thoughts that enter and dwell in our minds.

You may be surprised to see just how much of your precious and powerful mental energy is being wasted on causing suffering, when you could use it to actively reprogram yourself and move on from the unconscious programming you received as a child. In a way, positive self-talk is not some difficult and effortful task to master, but rather the shifting of all the ways your brain already maintains your self-concept, day after day.

In the chapters that follow, we'll explore exactly how to make the switch.

Takeaways

- It is easy to mistake positive self-talk for being vain, narcissistic, and shallow, overloading oneself with praise—but this is far from the case. Similarly, ignoring negative self-talk does not mean blinding yourself to your faults. Improving our self-talk is aimed at being more attuned with reality in a way that is conducive to achieving the goals we desire. Often we focus on the negative much more than the positive, and this distorts the reality of a situation. By practicing more positive self-talk, we're trying to get past this bias and

see things the way they are so that we can improve accordingly.
- There are many benefits of engaging in more positive self-talk. Several studies have looked into the matter and concluded that those who are more positive perform better at work and sports, are better at getting through challenging life circumstances, and have healthier relationships. Moreover, they also have a better self-image and feel good about themselves since they have a healthy sense of self.
- On the other hand, negative self-talk can be extremely damaging to our well-being. It releases cortisol in our bodies, compromising our immune function and preventing positive emotions from arising. Negative self-talk can also lead to a host of mental health issues such as depression, anxiety, panic disorders, and other undesirable outcomes like apathy, anger, self-pity, etc.
- If you're wondering where our self-talk styles originate from, the answer

is a host of factors that include our parenting, socio-cultural norms, our immediate environment, biology, our own biases and beliefs, among others. Many who have experienced strict or uncompromising home environments at a young age, or have routinely had their boundaries violated, come to adopt a low self-esteem, which in turn causes negative self-talk that can be hard to get rid of.

- These factors, along with experiences like bullying and different forms of abuse, also determine our self-esteem levels, which is the main determinant of whether our self-talk is negative or positive. As we understand why exactly our self-talk is the way it is, we can start to change and improve it to suit our needs.

- We end up with five levels of self-talk, each a higher amount of acceptance and self-esteem. Indeed, it starts with purely negative, then moves to aspirational, to positive, to a new identity, to newfound acceptance of both the negative and positive.

Chapter 3. All You Need to Do Is Listen

To engage in better self-talk, the first step is to identify and correct negative self-talk as it happens. It can sometimes be hard to distinguish between negative self-talk and self-criticism that can actually be conducive to growth. The goal here is to retain the latter while excluding the former so that we can attune ourselves to reality and improve our self-esteem.

Becoming aware of exactly when (and why) we address ourselves as we do is the only hope we have of stepping in and reclaiming our own inner landscape to create the reality we want for ourselves. All you need to do is listen, a much easier task than it seems.

The Key to Self-Awareness

Just because your self-talk is running unconsciously, doesn't mean that it's not having an effect on your life. Why not take conscious control of a process that is happening anyway? *Mindfulness* is a powerful way to gain awareness of our self-talk so we can bring it into the light of consciousness.

Clinical psychologist Dr. Mikaela Hildebrandt explains that there are two ways to relate to our thoughts, memories, opinions and perceptions: we can either stay *inside* this mental world and take it as a given, or we can step *outside* it, realizing that it is in fact our minds producing these thoughts and ideas. This is more or less the skill of metacognition, which is to be able to think about your thinking processes.

Mindfulness can help us shift from the former into the latter, taking a step back from our own mental chatter rather than fully identifying with it. It is the process wherein we consciously bring our attention toward our present experiences and thoughts while reserving all judgment to create genuine awareness of feelings or emotions. Research has shown that mindfulness can improve body image, relieve anxiety and depression, combat addictions, and support healthier lifestyle changes.

When we're mindful, we deliberately put ourselves in a conscious state where we are proactive rather than reactive. With a little mental distance, we can more easily accept the things that are beyond our control, and focus on those things that we can change.

Endlessly ruminating never gets us anywhere (it is staying trapped in level 1 and 2 self-talk) because we don't see our thoughts *as thoughts*. We assume those thoughts to be indicative of reality. Basically, we take our own word for it.

But if we are mindful, we notice ourselves thinking.

This helps us become aware of our thoughts without automatically having a negative or positive reaction to them. It allows us to evaluate and reflect upon those thoughts to see whether they actually have any merit. We can then choose to let go of judgments and criticisms, and even experiment with what it feels like to simply hold uncomfortable or negative sensations as they are, without leaping in with criticisms or doom-and-gloom thinking.

By being mindful, we give ourselves the time and space to untangle all those chaotic (and very damaging) self-talk messages we'd otherwise bombard ourselves with without a second thought. When we take on the perspective of a non-critical observer of our own thoughts, our awareness increases while our negative feelings decrease. We start to see how much of a *choice* it is to engage in tangled thought patterns. Perhaps most importantly, we introduce a space or pause between an initial reaction and a subsequent action.

Though we've spoken about the benefit of positive and healthy self-talk, the fact is that there is a lot to be gained from simply not engaging in negative self-talk. Negative self-talk does most damage when we are not aware of it, and don't acknowledge our own part in maintaining it.

By being mindful, we take the power away from negative self-talk and get enough distance to start imagining ways we could do things differently. If you think mindfulness merely entails you sitting around passively doing nothing, think again. Mindfulness is a powerful tool that helps us control what we focus on. It allows us to shift away from overwhelmingly negative emotions to hone in on something less threatening, like our breathing, sensory perceptions, bodily sensations, etc. Being mindful also cultivates a quality that's essential for all development and growth: curiosity.

When we are curious, we take on a proactive, interested perspective on life that moves us closer to acceptance and further from judgment. With an enquiring mind we can behold all our perceptive experience—good or bad—and simply sit with *what is*, without reacting, denying, clinging or trying to change anything.

When was the last time you watched your own thoughts with gentle curiosity? Can you sit with an open heart, willing to fully know whatever experience emerges? "Staying with" what happens within and without is a step toward not only awareness, but compassion for ourselves, wherever we are.

Mindfulness is the pause and the deep breath that allows us to ask: What is this? Can I let it be? Let it go? Watch it unfold?

Of course, sometimes you need to spring to action, but being mindful beforehand will allow you to develop the discernment needed to know exactly *when* to act, and when to yield. Practicing this way, we calmly step out of the whirlwind and torrent of stories, criticisms, judgments, worries and all the rest, strengthening our ability to self-regulate. What we are learning is mastery of our own attentive awareness, directing it to where *we* want it to go, rather than mindlessly chasing every distracting thought.

It helps us control our mind instead of letting it control us.

If you can deliberately and selectively focus on particular stimuli in your (inner and outer) environment, you are in effect shaping your world and your experience in it. Ask yourself where your attention usually goes—watch as it happens. What is the effect of this attention, and can you change it? This is the heart of mindfulness practice.

With mindfulness, you play with reprogramming your unfolding mind in *real time*, moment by moment. Don't watch yourself like a monitor, however, judging how well you are remaining aware or criticizing your mind for wandering. It's all grist for the mill—simply notice without judgment when your attention turns to negative self-talk. When you are aware, you can see previously unseen things— and allow yourself to change them, if you want. Neuroscientist Norman Farb found in a 2010 paper that meditators differed from non-meditators in their response to unpleasant emotions, showing less "cognitive elaboration" and an ability to more quickly move on. They felt their emotions as much as anyone, only they were not so carried away with them.

You don't need to embark on a strict meditation practice to be more mindful. Simply notice your thoughts. The following is a summary of *the 3-Minute Responsive Breathing Space* from Zindel Segal et al., 2012:

Rest in a comfortable position, either lying down or sitting upright. The exercise consists of three steps, each lasting a minute each. See what emotions arise, and notice how they play out on your body, in your breath, in your mind. Don't rush—just sit with what's there. Notice what catches your attention and choose to stay with it, bringing back your focus if it wanders. Then, narrow your field of attention to just your breathing and block out everything else. Do this for about a minute before expanding your field of attention to include your body and any sensations that you might be feeling.

Like many mindfulness exercises, Segal intended this practice to be a way for one to check in with one's own thoughts and then move on from them by first narrowing, followed by expanding our focus. After a few minutes, reflect on the experience:

where did this thought or emotion come from? What does it do to you? Do you want to go deeper into it, or do you want to let it go and put your attention elsewhere?

If it seems complicated, it isn't—but it takes practice and willingness. Throughout your day, pause, take a breath and watch your inner landscape, using the following prompts to guide you:

1. What thoughts, feelings or sensations am I paying attention to?
2. Is my attention in my thoughts, emotions, body, or all three?
3. When did I start attending? How did I start and how is the sensation changing over time?
4. What is the nature of my attention— am I stuck in a loop, curious, focused, daydreamy, fantasizing, or focused in on one tiny detail?

The more you practice mindfulness, the more you'll become aware of your own thinking patterns. Question number 4 above asks about the quality of your conscious awareness, what your attention is resting on, and how. But if you've spent a long time unconscious of your own thinking, these questions can be difficult to answer.

Here are some styles of thinking or common mental patterns that you might notice—see if you recognize any in yourself, in order to get a more concrete grasp on them the next time you encounter them!

- Black and white thinking

This is thinking in extremes with no room for nuance or gray area (or compassion!). For example, "he used to be The One, but now I see he's the worst person in the world" or "I'd better do this perfectly or I might as well give up forever." Watch out for all-or-nothing, zero-sum, high-stakes thinking and words like "always," "never" or "must." Black and white thinking is a common defense mechanism that we typically use when we are unable to grasp the complexities of a particular situation, person, etc. Though this can help us feel less anxious, it inevitably leads us to distorted views of reality.

You might see what happens if you soften these statements to make them more subtle—"He and I don't get on anymore, but we did have some good times together" or "I'll do my best with this and it's not the end of the world if I make a few mistakes."

- Catastrophizing

If you're mentally stuck thinking of worse and worse possible outcomes, you'll know what catastrophizing feels like—and how easy it is to get carried away with it! "If I don't do well in this exam, I'll definitely fail and not only will everyone else think I'm an idiot, I'll fall further and further behind and I'll have to graduate late, and I'll never get a real job, and I'll be broke and unhappy forever, and my parents will be so disappointed and…"

Try telling yourself that bad things might happen, but so what? Can you stay in the moment, right here, where everything is actually just fine? One of the reasons why we feel tempted to catastrophize is that we implicitly believe our worrying over an outcome will actively protect us from experiencing it. However, the opposite is true. It only makes that outcome more likely, and remembering that can help us refrain from engaging in this type of negative self-talk.

- Filtering

Filtering involves excluding all positives while focusing overwhelmingly on negative details, as if you were wearing glasses that filtered out the good and emphasized the bad. You deliver a brilliant speech but trip slightly on your way down from the podium. You forget everything you did right and zoom in on the one thing you did wrong. You have put a negative filter on your experience.

- Overgeneralizing

Related to this is taking one distinct experience and assuming it applies to every other experience. You tripped coming off a podium once and now tell yourself "I always mess up speeches." You get dumped once and decide that every person of the opposite sex hates you as well.

- Mind reading

Your boss doesn't greet you as you walk past her in the canteen. You think, "she probably hates me." You end a first date convinced the other person finds you awful, despite a lack of evidence. Every time we assume we know others' thoughts, motivations or feelings, we risk interjecting our own. Like black and white thinking, mind reading is often a response to uncertainty, which is instinctively mitigated with negative thoughts.

- Emotional Reasoning

As the name suggests, this cognitive distortion involves jumping to certain irrational conclusions based on just your emotions. This happens when we assume that feeling a certain way means that we really must be the thing we feel. So if we fail a test and feel like an idiot or failure, we conclude from this that we actually are those things, even if there isn't any evidence to support it beyond individual outcomes.

Stop and double-check the evidence in front of you. Trust that people say what they mean, and mean what they say. Look to see what core beliefs of your *own* are being reflected back at you.

As you can imagine, all five of these patterns can be combined. For example, someone is asked to babysit their nephew one evening but nervously thinks "I never get this kind of thing right, I'm not good with kids, I'm the worst auntie ever (black and white thinking). I bet they only asked me because they couldn't get their normal babysitter (mind reading). My sister and brother-in-law *always* do this, always put me in these difficult situations (overgeneralization). I bet I totally mess up and the kid sets himself on fire or something (catastrophizing)."

In this example, the woman might have also conveniently forgotten the time she already babysat her nephew with no problems at all—definite filtering!

Assessment Tools and Tips

As you become more and more aware of that voice that appears inside you and exactly what it says, you'll become better at appraising its accuracy. If you're just starting out, you may believe you don't even have self-talk—but look closer and you'll notice it soon enough. Some self-talk is obvious, but often the more insidious type slips under the radar, and needs your conscious awareness to be detected.

Slowing down and deliberately asking yourself what you're thinking can make your self-talk more apparent and tangible in the moment. You could do this by practicing the mindfulness exercise above, or you could notice yourself feeling upset, triggered, or stressed, and decide to write out your thoughts in a journal.

By writing things down, you can see your more transient thoughts on the page, and understand that a lot of what you think of as an irrefutable fact of life really isn't. Journaling, speaking out loud or meditating help you see your *thoughts as thoughts*, so you can step outside your mind for a moment and take control of your beliefs, rather than letting them control you. While writing your thoughts down, the psychologist David Burns recommends making three columns where you first write your negative thoughts, identifying the negative thinking pattern (like the ones mentioned above) that is at play, and coming up with a rational response to your original thoughts as an effective way to make self-talk more positive.

Get into the habit of asking yourself, "Is what I'm thinking really true? Is it a provable fact or merely a belief/worry/rumination/assumption?" More often than not, the answer will be immediately apparent to you.

Don't take your own word for it—look for evidence. You might think "those people over there are laughing at me, they must think I look stupid," but by pausing for a second you soon see that there's zero reason to believe this. If you can see a thought is irrational and causing you upset, you give yourself the chance to drop it. You'll also recognize that your assumption is a result of trying to read minds, a cognitive distortion we've covered above.

You could also seek alternative explanations. The people might be laughing at a joke someone has shared, and they may not have even noticed you. By not going along with your worst and most irrational assumptions, you give yourself the chance to pursue other, healthier trains of thought. You can check this by noticing how you feel once you examine other possibilities.

In time, you can use any instance of self-talk as a helpful clue that points to your negative underlying beliefs about yourself and the world. You could arrive at some of these hidden but powerful beliefs by asking, "if this thought were true, what would it imply about me or the world?"

You may answer this question with, "It would mean I was an inferior/ridiculous/stupid/wrong/bad person"—demonstrating that as we've discussed, the root of harmful self-talk is poor self-esteem or a deeply held core belief in our own lack of worth. In such cases, what might help is assuming the answer (being stupid, wrong, etc.) to be true, and asking yourself, "Would it be the end of the world if it was true?" and "If it's true, what can I do to change that?" Realizing that something isn't as bad as we initially thought makes us doubt the truth of the claim itself, helping us discard negative and unhelpful thoughts in the process.

By becoming aware of and examining our self-talk, our thoughts will lead us to the underlying beliefs from which they spring. Crucially, we can start to dismantle them—the next time we see the belief rear its head, we can ask ourselves if we'd like to entertain it or let it fade away in favor of a healthier, more objective one.

In time, you can start to notice your own unique patterns, and work consistently to reprogram old beliefs with ones that better serve you. You begin the work of choosing your attitude, rather than having your beliefs operate silently against you in the background of your awareness.

Ask yourself the following questions to guide you closer to your own unique patterns of self-talk:

- Am I using black-and-white terms?
- Am I expecting perfection?
- Am I jumping to conclusions?
- Am I exaggerating anything or blowing anything out of proportion?
- Am I only focusing on the negative side?
- Am I being irrational or illogical in my conclusions?
- Am I taking things personally when I shouldn't?
- What feelings are beneath my current thoughts?
- What does this thought say about my deep beliefs?
- Ultimately, are these thoughts having a helpful or hurtful effect on me?

Awareness is half the battle won. But the other half is learning to consistently challenge negative core beliefs as you unearth them, so they can be replaced. When you're starting out, you may be tempted to cling even more tightly to a negative belief. You may not be willing to accept alternatives, or you may believe that you have more evidence for a negative belief than you really do.

You need to systematically (and compassionately) challenge yourself. Think of it as a debate with yourself, and try coming up with points that undermine the narrative in your mind. Eventually, this will become habitual when you experience negative self-talk.

You might find that *some* of your thoughts are actually true, or at least partly true. Others will be wildly exaggerated or completely false. But when you're upset, how do you know which is which?

Properly appraising your self-talk is not very different from constructing a convincing and logical argument. Imagine yourself trying to poke holes in irrational narratives like a lawyer or scientist would, looking for hard evidence and dismissing unfounded assumptions.

There are a few tips and techniques to help you do this:

Imagine how someone else may think about this same situation. Picture a close friend, confidante, or admired mentor and how they would approach the same idea. You could also imagine saying your thought out loud to someone you love—this will very quickly show you if a thought is needlessly unkind!

Anchor in reality. Ask yourself, "How do I know this will happen? Is there really any evidence this thought is true? What else could happen instead, and how likely is it? What are the actual facts here?" Notice if you're assuming you already have the answer when you don't, or are attempting to predict the future when it's not possible. Become curious about what's happened before and its relationship to the current moment. Look at how sure you feel about certain self-talk statements and ask whether your perspective is founded. Grounding in reality means taking a step back and distinguishing between fact and fantasy. It may sometimes be helpful to simply say, "I haven't got enough information to make a judgment just yet" instead of assuming the worst.

Look at the thought itself and ask whether it's doing you any good to hold it. How does it make you feel, and do you want to feel that way? Is the thought helpful in any way?

De-catastrophize your thinking. Ask what's the worst that can happen, and whether it's really all that bad. Let's say people *are* laughing at you—does it really matter all that much? Is it the end of the world? Most things we worry about won't matter in a month, let alone a year. Ask yourself whether the thing you're ruminating about will last forever, to gain perspective. Try to remember that good things might happen too—have you included them in your ruminations?

Consider alternatives, and entertain the possibility that things could go better than expected. You might decide you need to find more information—often, anxiety and low self-esteem worsen in uncertainty, but disappear when you have more objective and empowering information at hand. Try to open your thinking to allow in other thoughts, explanations, appraisals, and predictions. Put on the brain of someone else and look at the issue again. If all else fails, you can often halt negative self-talk in its tracks simply by recognizing you're doing it and committing to stepping away from the problem until you feel calmer and ready to tackle the situation again.

Of course, this isn't always possible. We're all human and thus prone to making terrible mistakes that really can be every bit as bad as we think them to be. In such cases, it is important to not beat ourselves up. Instead, we must look to learn and improve from our missteps in the future. With the right attitude, even the worst negatives can be turned into something positive. By regulating our self-talk, we can ensure that our mistakes don't become a damning indictment of who we are, and how we view ourselves.

Assessing your self-talk entirely in your mind can become taxing and convoluted given the sheer number of thoughts we experience at any given moment. To make things easier, there are several activities you can choose from to help you evaluate and improve your self-talk.

First, you can try the paper clip technique: in the morning, put a handful of paper clips in your right-hand pocket and, whenever you become aware of yourself engaging in negative self-talk, switch one of the paper clips over to the left-hand pocket. At the end of the day, you'll have a record of how frequent your negative self-talk really is. This is a great technique if you've already identified a common pattern and want to keep track of it, but it's not enough to reveal the content of your self-talk.

If you'd like a more detailed log of your self-talk, keep a journal where you jot down the thoughts every time you notice one pop up. Include the date, whether the thought was positive or negative, what events triggered it, and the thought itself. You may also choose to rate individual thoughts based on how rational they really are. When you see yourself realizing that many of them aren't, and that you yourself see them as irrational, they will inevitably bother you less. You can also include any core beliefs you can connect them to, and a gentle alternative thought. Journaling self-talk allows you to more clearly spot patterns, but does take more time to do.

Choose a journaling technique that works for you and your lifestyle. You might try using a short journaling technique wherein you only rate your self-talk on a scale at various points in the day, giving you quantitative data over time about how the tone of your self-talk is changing. This can be helpful if you're using another dedicated practice to improve self-talk, but would like to track the results and improvement over the long term.

Another clever technique is to not wait until you naturally experience negative self-talk, but deliberately try to summon it through visualization and mental imagery. Close your eyes, vividly imagine a challenging scenario and walk yourself through it, watching to see the thoughts that spring to mind as you do. This is also a great way to rehearse alternatives, working through the same situation again but with a different set of thoughts, noticing how you feel.

Finally, you might decide rather than keeping track of your self-talk, to more directly monitor your overall self-concept and self-esteem. After all, this is the layer at which we hope to make the most profound changes—a healthy sense of self is always the goal of improving self-talk.

How do you know whether your self-esteem has actually improved?

The most obvious way is to go by how you feel, and you may with time notice that your self-talk is shifting to better reflect a sense of self-respect and value. If you'd like a more quantitative measure, however, there are many tests and psychological inventories designed to put an exact figure on various aspects of your self-concept.

These tests all have different theoretical underpinnings but will give you a handy way of tracking progress over time. Many of them are short and can be found online.

The Personal Self-Concept Questionnaire (PSQ) created by Goñi, Madariaga, Axpe & Goñi (2011) measures things like autonomy, self-fulfillment, and emotional self-concept. You will need to rate your agreement with a series of 22 statements on a scale of 1 to 5, to get a total score.

Saraswat's Self-Concept Questionnaire (SCQ) is older (published 1984) but still popular, and measures self-concept over six areas: physical, social, temperamental, educational, moral and intellectual. Counselor Susan Harrill's Self-Esteem Inventory is more specifically aimed at measuring self-esteem using 25 statements that you respond to with a rating between 0 and 4.

These scales (and there are many, many others available—a quick Google search will return dozens of options) will give you a rough idea of where you stand. It's important to use the same one if you intend to compare measurements over time. If a full-on psych assessment seems unnecessary, try other activities to get a snapshot of your self-esteem as it stands.

Make art, doodle, mind map, or journal to answer the question "who am I?" and cover your likes, dislikes, strengths, weaknesses, values and so on. Reflect on compliments you've received, on your self-talk and your goals with it, your progresses and challenges. Generally, it's advisable to measure your self-esteem through the things that are intrinsic to you, rather than external factors such as your wealth, appearance, your career, etc. All of these are subject to change with time and circumstances, but the best indicator of healthy self-esteem is that it remains constant through thick and thin.

Re-read previous negative self-talk statements and see if they still resonate, notice if you're more comfortable receiving compliments, or take note if you feel better about yourself in general. This will give you a more qualitative look at how healthy your self-concept is.

Takeaways

- The first step to recognizing and correcting your inner voice is to become aware of it. A powerful way to do this is through practicing mindfulness. Mindfulness is the activity wherein you train your mind

to become aware of your present emotions, sensations, or experience and accept them without clouding them with any judgment.
- There are many different mindfulness activities you can follow. One of them is called the three-minute breathing space and it proceeds in three steps, as follows. First, simply take in all your thoughts and observe them without attempting to control their flow. Then, narrow your focus away from them and simply concentrate on your breathing for a minute. Lastly, expand your focus to include your body and physical sensations. Activities like these help you recognize your thoughts and move on from them without overthinking.
- As you practice mindfulness, you will become aware of some negative thinking patterns that we commonly engage in. One of them is called black and white thinking, where we mislead ourselves into looking at the world in strictly binary terms.

Another is catastrophizing, which involves drawing exaggerated conclusions from comparatively minor incidents. Patterns like these distort our thinking and obscure the nature of reality.

- Journaling is a powerful tool for not only recognizing negative thought patterns, but also challenging them to come up with more rational and thought-out alternatives. Writing your thoughts makes them seem more tangible, and allows you to evaluate them better than when it's all in your head.
- However, if journaling doesn't sound suitable to you, there are other ways to assess your self-talk. Reflect on your negative thoughts and core beliefs as they come to you and compassionately, but systematically challenge them. Play the role of a lawyer and look for logical holes. Try to identify the thinking patterns that are distorting your self-talk, and work on replacing them with healthier thoughts.

Chapter 4. Replace, Transform, Evolve

This is the chapter where all our self-awareness, focused intention, and consistent effort culminate in changes to our self-concept that can concretely improve every area of life.

Cognitive Behavior Therapy (CBT) is an effective framework for organizing attempts to reprogram your self-talk, thought by thought. It's typically practiced with a psychotherapist or counselor, but the principles are accessible and can be applied on your own—in fact, some of the exercises in the previous sections have been informal examples of CBT exercises.

CBT can address a whole range of life problems, but is particularly suited for understanding and changing underlying core beliefs in a systematic way. CBT techniques help you identify and take control of certain mental processes, cope with stress and adversity, resolve conflicts, and deal with grief, illness, trauma and more. When practiced regularly, CBT can also induce changes in brain chemistry that were once thought possible only through medication. As such, improvements that result from CBT are highly likely to be long lasting, since they can fundamentally alter the way our minds function.

While the risks associated with CBT are minimal, it's worth being prepared to face some potentially uncomfortable feelings, or confront difficult beliefs and fears. Most importantly, CBT won't magically make life's problems go away. Rather, it will teach you to better cope with them, and to face challenges with empowered autonomy and the self-confidence needed to cope and thrive.

CBT doesn't always work (and it's OK if it doesn't!), but you can improve your chances of success by:

- Opting to work with a counselor or at least sharing your journey with someone you trust.
- Being willing to be open and honest with yourself—embarrassment and denial will only get in the way.
- Being dedicated. We may be convinced that our own case is hopeless and beyond repair, but CBT takes time and consistent effort to work. Bear in mind that there are no miraculous overnight results, and half-hearted attempts here and there are unlikely to have lasting effects.

Three-Step Cognitive Behavioral Therapy

CBT is evidence-based and well-suited to tackling the inner dialogue that accompanies worry, anxiety, regret, shame, grief, guilt, blame and low self-esteem. Life is filled with challenges, adversities, and unexpected events. These can either be viewed as painful and unfair, or manageable and growth-inspiring—all depending on the mindset we cultivate with our self-talk.

CBT is not about "thinking positively" but thinking more clearly, realistically, and neutrally—without cognitive distortions. In CBT, our thoughts, feelings, and behavior are all interconnected, i.e. if we can change our thoughts, we can change our feelings and consequently how we act (and vice versa).

We've covered some cognitive distortions already—catastrophizing, black and white thinking, etc.—and have begun recognizing the language of negative self-talk in ourselves. Observing your thinking and becoming aware of previously automatic thoughts and distortions is step 1.

Step 2 is learning to gently and consistently challenge these thoughts and their underlying core beliefs, testing just how accurate they are. We considered this in the previous chapter where we asked ourselves questions, tested our assumptions, and encouraged ourselves to seek alternatives.

Step 3 is doing the work of replacing these distorted thoughts and beliefs with ones that are healthier, more accurate, and more likely to lead to a balanced and optimistic life. Before we move on to this very important step, however, we need to look a little closer at the language of negative self-talk, and how to spot triggers and warning signs so that we can step in and stop cognitive distortions *before* they take flight in our minds.

Step 1: Observe

Self-talk is made of words. That's all it is.

It's literally like a film script that you run internally. But words can be edited, deleted, rewritten. In previous sections, we've focused on fact vs. fiction, and the importance of comparing our thoughts against objective reality as much as possible. This is a way of fine-tuning the *content* of our thoughts, but there's also the question of the style, grammar, vocabulary and tone of the language we use when we talk to ourselves.

You've utterly failed, you big fat idiot.

You didn't pass the quiz that time.

Both of these statements can refer to the same event, and in a way are factually equivalent—i.e. "didn't pass" is the same as "failed." However, it's obvious that they carry very different emotional nuances, and will have very different effects on the person thinking them.

Automatic, negative self-talk has a certain flavor that you can recognize with practice. It's usually short, spontaneous and emotionally loaded with strong words, or has a rambling, looping quality. It's filled with overgeneralizing language like *always, never, nobody, should, nothing, must, completely*, or language filled with guilt, self-flagellation and judgment.

Watch for language that spirals or feeds on itself or steadily mounts in intensity. Look out for thoughts that you accept as true immediately in the moment without a second thought. Automatic thoughts are usually strongly infused with feelings of fear, anger or shame, and will appear in language that suggests this—at the very least, you'll know it's negative self-talk simply because you feel awful when you listen to it!

Step 2: Challenge

If you catch yourself in negative self-talk—congratulations. Even better, however, would be to avoid it altogether, or stop it before it happens using your knowledge of what usually triggers these thoughts for you. Negative thoughts are easier to recognize and handle when they are still small.

As a technique, "thought stopping" appeared in the late 1950s in the sport psychology world, and was used to cut short self-defeating and anxious thoughts that got in the way of performance. An excellent overview can be found in Zinsser, Bunker and Williams' 2010 book, *Cognitive Techniques for Building Confidence and Enhancing Performance.* The idea is to use a behavioral or mental cue to snap out of a negative self-talk spiral.

For those suffering from mental health issues like panic disorders, it can be especially hard to distract yourself once a negative thought appears in your mind. This technique acts as a tool to help become aware of and then replace these thoughts in a way similar to practicing mindfulness.

Pinching yourself, imagining a red light or saying "stop" out loud can all act as cues to bring your conscious awareness to the moment and away from negative self-talk.

It's essentially the art of beneficial distraction, and even more effective when you then quickly redirect your attention to a preferable subject (a more realistic thought, perhaps?) It's an assertive stance you are taking against that inner dialogue that you know only carries you to places you don't want to go.

The technique can potentially backfire if you end up constantly monitoring yourself to look for failures you can pounce on—the trick is to bring mindfulness to the process, not punishment or judgment. If you try this technique for a while and find it actually worsens the problem, ease up, be more compassionate, or simply attempt a different technique. Thought stopping may help for more superficial rumination, but not for deeper anxieties that may respond better to slow, deliberate engagement.

If you'd like to try the technique, however, here's how to begin:

Write down a list of all the most distressing, recurring, distracting and unwanted thoughts you wish to stop paying attention to. Try to rank them from most to least distressing. Include anything from "one day my boss is going to figure out how inept I am and fire me" to "this lump probably means cancer."

Next, do some prep work by practicing—sit alone in a private room and spend some time visualizing any situation in life where the most distressing thought might conceivably intrude. For a while, go into the thought and focus on it, feeling out its contours. Then, as abruptly as you can, stop the thought.

Stand up quickly, say "stop!" out loud, snap your eyes open, make a loud clapping noise or click your fingers. Empty your mind and try to hold that emptiness for thirty seconds or so. If the thought tries to intrude again, repeat "stop" as often as necessary.

What you are trying to do is gain practice at stopping rumination mid-thought. In time you can be less drastic with your interruption, and eventually internalize the "stop" so you only say it quietly to yourself. You don't necessarily need to use the word *stop*—you could also visualize your thoughts as traffic that stops dutifully at a red light. Try saying out loud "I'm having a thought about XYZ right now" to remind yourself that it's just a thought, and to gain distance.

Whatever you do, simply remind yourself that thoughts are just words—just a script that you can stop in its tracks and rewrite. The hard work is to recognize the thought, but once you do, realize it has no hold on you unless you pay attention to it. Make a habit of using certain phrases to interrupt unwanted thoughts, divert your attention and affirm your *choice* to follow certain thoughts and drop others:

Don't go there

Let it be

Let it go

It's in the past

Leave it alone

Focus

Don't pay attention

Slow down

This, too, will pass

It doesn't matter

Breathe

You've got this***

Using this thought stopping technique may make some people uncomfortable—aren't you just ignoring your problems?

It's worth remembering that thought stopping is best used for those thoughts that you know are intrusive, unwanted, and genuinely unhelpful. These are the thoughts that you have already identified as irrational, untrue, or exaggerated, and you know that entertaining them will only lead to stress and worry.

Your goal is to tolerate and manage anxiety, rather than turn a blind eye to it. Similarly, having thought stopping in your mental toolkit doesn't mean you are unable to hear your own intuition or engage when a situation warrants genuine concern. Thought stopping is merely a mental fuse that lets you halt catastrophic rumination before you get too carried away with it.

For some people, the thought-stopping technique outlined above may feel a little punitive and may not work for them. Thankfully, there are plenty of other techniques underpinned by the same principles. You could try scattered counting, for example. Counting to ten is a common anger management technique, but it's easy enough to become automatic, allowing your brain to carry on ruminating even as you count. Rather, jump around with random numbers to engage your thoughts more, e.g. "43, 12, 5, 88, 356, 90, 5…"

In the same way, a mantra or spoken word can interrupt runaway thoughts—choose a more complicated nonsense phrase or something in another language to prevent yourself from doing it too automatically. Alternatively, you can select affirmations based on your specific triggers or perceived negative qualities. Though they can take time to work, the reason so many find them effective is that our brains eventually come to think of them as true. These affirmations can be specific quotes from religious texts, or statements like "I believe in myself" and "I am in charge of my thoughts." These can be recited both mentally and out loud, but with conviction. Repeating lines you don't really believe will be pointless, so choose your affirmations wisely.

You could try self-soothing with encouraging positive self-talk, such as "don't worry, you can handle this" or "you're doing great!" Play a song you like or listen to a podcast to engage your auditory channels and pull attention away from anxious overthinking.

A distracting cue can also be physical in nature—physically move yourself into a different position, get up and do a few jumping jacks or go for a quick jog outside to break out of thought loops. You can also switch to more bodily/somatic awareness by simply focusing on your breath, and practicing a technique called muscle isolation.

Sit or lie comfortably, close your eyes, and then work your way through all your muscles, starting from the ones in your toes. Squeeze them as tightly as you can for five seconds and then release and relax completely. Then focus on the muscles in your feet and legs, moving up until you reach the muscles in your face and scalp. Not only will this help immensely to release physical tension, but it will distract your overactive mind and bring it more fully into the present moment.

Muscle isolation can be an excellent warmup to a more formal sitting meditation practice, or a great way to end a mindfulness session. Combine it with gentle soothing music or head outside where you can feel the sun and breeze on your skin.

Another classic CBT technique is to decide that instead of stopping or running away from scary and overwhelming thoughts, you'll simply stare them down and ask what's the worst that could happen. Look squarely at your ruminations and say, *so what?* It's rarely as bad as you think, and seldom something you truly cannot handle. Research has found that even those who lose their limbs or eyesight—suffering tragedies anyone would consider horrifying—soon return to a median level of happiness because of how powerful our modes of adaptation are. As such, no matter what it is you're worried over, you're very likely to be able to survive it just fine even if the event were to occur.

You might like to visualize yourself actually encountering the worst-case scenario with grace and poise, tackling the problem and seeing that it isn't in fact the end of the world, even if the worst does come to pass. This alone can take the steam out of your most catastrophic ruminations.

Step 3: Replace

Some thoughts are so useless and untrue that they can be discarded immediately, or stopped using any of the techniques described above. With practice, you'll be able to recognize totally harmful thoughts (like, "I'm probably going to die" or "everyone hates me") and release them immediately.

Some ideas and thoughts, however, are a little more subtle and are more appropriately rewritten rather than discarded entirely. These thoughts are often those that we believe have a grain of truth to them. Here, it's necessary to practice a degree of conscious discernment to determine what kind of life script will serve you best. Again, this is a step that can only be done *after* you've gained a good awareness of the kinds of self-talk you engage in—otherwise you risk having these techniques exacerbate rather than solve the problem.

Exercise 1: Think it through

This exercise takes some time and effort. The first step is to note down your self-talk using any of the methods already discussed (for example, by using a bullet journal, writing down your core beliefs or periodically taking a self-esteem inventory). Then, after a week, try to look for particular themes or patterns.

What kind of self-talk is it (for example catastrophizing or mindreading)?

What events, thoughts, feelings, people, or situations triggered the self-talk?

What common threads can you identify?

What was the effect or result of these thoughts?

What do they say about your core beliefs?

Reflect on what you see. Get some distance on your thoughts. This way, we're more likely to evaluate them truthfully, as opposed to in the moment when our feelings might cloud our judgement. Notice if your self-talk has actually held you back in life or made you feel bad. Ask yourself, how would it feel to have positive self-talk instead? What might your life look like and what could you achieve if you didn't limit yourself in this way?

In thinking through things carefully, the more positive alternative is likely to appear to you. For example, you may see that you constantly exaggerate physical symptoms and then get stuck in doom-and-gloom thought loops about what might happen if you fall ill. Seeing all this objectively noted on paper, seeing how it negatively impacts your life in many ways, and seeing how utterly irrational it is, you slowly begin to loosen the self-talk's hold on you.

By completing this exercise, you can begin to see the more accurate and realistic options available to you. Better yet, when you try them out and monitor yourself for a week, you may be surprised to learn just how much wasted mental energy and anguish you can avoid by consciously and deliberately dropping negative self-talk.

Exercise 2: Change channels

The previous exercise is a gentle way of supporting yourself as you naturally find your way to healthier cognitive alternatives. But you might need something a little more direct, especially for those core beliefs that are more persistent.

You can do this exercise alone or add it onto the Think it Through exercise above, and it's essentially what you would do with a CBT therapist. Write down a negative thought as it pops up. Now, deliberately reword the sentence in front of you until it is more neutral and objective.

- Remove all-or-nothing language like *never, everybody, none,* etc.
- Remove emotive and harsh language like *idiot, hate, fail, disgusting,* etc. Replace the word "difficult" or "impossible" with "challenging" and use "annoyed" instead of "angry." Use

language that is more time-limited, for example "I'm feeling sad today" rather than "I'm sad," which implies a permanent state of affairs.

- Make the tone more neutral and compassionate.
- Instead of saying "can't" try saying "don't." Own your preferences and the place you're currently in. Rather than saying "I can't do it" simply say "I don't do it" or even "I don't want to do it." This doesn't shut off the possibility of doing it later; it's just a statement of fact, whereas "I can't" sets a hard limit.
- Similarly, avoid hedging language like "I'll try" or "maybe" or "I guess I could…" Speak directly and state what you'll do.
- Remove any outright falsehoods or attempts to mindread or predict the future.
- Phrase things gently and compassionately, as though you were speaking to a loved one or even a person in a professional context.

- You might like to add some positive phrases like the ones already covered earlier (e.g. *you've got this*).
- Remove assumptions and unsupported conclusions. You might try replacing these statements simply with "I don't have enough information yet," which is far more neutral and accurate.
- If you can, rephrase statements as questions. Instead of saying something is impossible, ask *how* it could be possible.
- Likewise, see if you can switch focus entirely and reframe things to the positive: instead of identifying limitations and problems, pinpoint resources, options, alternatives, and possibilities.
- Put the words in the mouth of a trusted mentor and loved one and see how they fit—what would they say instead? How would they phrase things?

Here are some examples:

Negative: "I embarrassed myself in front of all those people and they'll never ask me to do a presentation ever again."

Positive: "That didn't go as I planned but it's OK. I did my best and learnt a lot, and will prepare better for next time. It's not the end of the world if I receive some constructive feedback from my bosses."

Negative: "Who would want to have a relationship with an old, unattractive person like me? There's no point dating, nobody would look twice."

Positive: "I have no evidence that trying to meet someone new would be impossible. I deserve a loving relationship, so I'm going to put myself out there. Whatever happens, I can love and respect myself."

Negative: "It's hopeless starting a business in this economy, you'll only fail."

Positive: "I have faith in myself and a lot to offer. There are always options, and I'm going to do my best and keep a positive attitude."

After you've changed a statement, deliberately make an effort to redirect your attention toward this new version instead of more negative statements. You can combine this with thought stopping, halting the negative thought and then redirecting to your reworded script instead. Practice makes perfect, i.e. the more you tell your brain something, the more it believes it's true!

Exercise 3: Testing for accuracy

Some self-talk has been going on so long that it's become embedded in layer upon layer of assumptions, even becoming part of our identity and worldview. These beliefs take time to dismantle! Learning to get to the root of a statement's objective accuracy sounds easy, but it's definitely a skill that takes time and effort to master.

- Is your self-talk fact or opinion?
- Where does this idea really come from?

- What is the evidence and what assumptions have you made?
- Can you think of any counterexamples to disprove this idea?

Testing for accuracy can be as simple as noticing yourself say "nobody thinks my art is any good" and changing it to "I haven't shown many people my work, but I do remember that nice compliment I got once." Even the smallest positive that is demonstrably and objectively true can act as a counterweight to a whole universe of negative thinking that actually has no proof to support it at all.

Remember, you don't have to go to the other extreme—the goal of positive self-talk is not to become a narcissist who is incapable of accurately seeing their own faults. Rather, you are seeking moderation, balance, and a realistic and healthy viewpoint. You'll be surprised by how unremarkable "healthy" self-talk sounds in comparison to what you're used to!

You can use these re-scripting techniques in the moment you have a negative thought, or you can do it more systematically, for example at the end of a day when you sit down with a journal and reflect. You might include some mindfulness and guided meditation, too.

To commit to shifting to your more positive self-talk phrases, pin new phrases and affirmations to a wall or visible place. Start the morning by reading through them or regularly take five-minute breaks throughout the day to check in with yourself, breathe, and recalibrate, using these statements as cues.

All of these techniques can be used in combination. For example, someone might keep a self-talk diary for two weeks where they note down the thoughts that emerge as well as the triggers, results, and accompanying emotions that go with these thoughts.

They soon see a pattern: that much of their self-talk can be boiled down to the core belief "I'm not as good as everyone else" and that the low self-esteem behind this belief expresses itself in mindreading ruminations. For example, "They said they liked my shoes but I'm sure they think they're hideous and were just lying to make me feel better…"

Reflecting on this, the person decides that self-defeating attitudes like this one have only served to undermine them all through life, and that they are ready to embrace a more realistic, compassionate outlook toward themselves. They note down a range of thoughts that pop into their head throughout the day and then systematically ask whether they're all that true.

Is it *really* true that you are a failure? Maybe it's more accurate to say that you didn't do as well as you thought you would on one particular task, but that your overall performance is great. Is it *really* true that other people are sitting whispering amongst themselves about how awful you are? Far more likely is that people barely notice you and your missteps, because they are far too busy dealing with their own!

By gradually testing the truth of the self-talk we are increasingly aware of, we realize how many other options there are. We can try to rewrite some of the most commonly occurring thoughts and themes, with improved alternatives:

"They don't like me" turns into "They don't know me, but there's no reason for them not to like me."

"I'm falling behind in life" becomes "I'm doing the best I can and I'm on my own path. I don't have to compete with anyone."

"Everyone else is so much more talented compared to me" is reworded into "I admire the skills of others, but that doesn't mean I don't have good points of my own. Besides, I'm willing to learn."

These rewritten statements can be pulled out or recalled when the person spots themselves falling into a detrimental thinking spiral again. They can use the "stop" technique to halt negative self-talk in its tracks, then redirect. They can build in moments of meditation and self-reflection throughout the day, regularly using positive statements like, "you're just fine" and "don't go down that path" when negative self-talk rears its head. Here is one potential internal monologue:

"You're such a loser, you're doing all this stupid positive self-talk stuff and you know it'll never work, that's for other people, but you'll just mess it up. Besides, it's not negative self-talk, it's the truth—you really are a loser... STOP. Take a deep breath. Remember, these are just thoughts, not reality. I recognize this pattern. This is my inner critic and I've already decided I don't care what they say. You're doing great. Breathe. Now look at the situation again and make a conscious decision about your inner script. You're *not* a loser, you're working hard on your self-esteem and that's admirable. It will work with time. *It probably won't.* STOP. I already know what lies down that path, and I'm not biting. I'm going outside for a run..."

If the above stream of consciousness seems a little extreme to you, consider this: your mind is *always* running a script very much like the one above, but it may be conscious or unconscious. If it's unconscious, it will run along unawares, quietly affecting every aspect of your life. But if you can make it conscious, you can change it, and reap the benefits. It's your choice.

Though we've uncovered several different techniques and approaches to help you unravel unhelpful self-talk and gradually replace it with healthier core beliefs and supportive inner dialogue, the process is likely to be a lot more ad hoc in real life.

What's important is that your approach works for *you*. Try a few things and give them time to work, but don't be afraid of tweaking these methods to your own ends, combining them or trying something completely different.

Other helpful tips to keep in mind as you master the art of re-scripting your inner mental world:

- Do re-scripting work when you're calm and feeling optimistic, and not when you're stuck in the middle of a mental storm or feeling upset.

- Keep at it—it's better to do a little and often than expect that one session will solve everything forever!

- Run through your new script even if you don't quite believe it at first—with repetition, your brain will soon start to literally rewire itself.

- Don't be afraid to make changes to your script—you might not get it right the first time. Remember, it doesn't have to be over-the-top enthusiastic and unrealistically positive. It just has to be neutral and relatively unbiased.

- It's up to you to evaluate your script as you go. How does the new self-talk feel? What effects does it have on your mood, your self-concept, and your behavior?

- Don't beat yourself up if occasionally you end up ranting, complaining or going down a stress rabbit hole—it's perfectly normal to be grumpy or pessimistic at times. Likewise, a little stress or criticism isn't the end of the world. Just keep things in perspective and try whenever possible to return to awareness of your thoughts *as thoughts*.

The language of positive self-talk flows naturally from a healthy self-concept. But if you're trying to undo the damage of a poor self-esteem, you may find yourself upgrading your negative self-talk in the hopes that it positively influences your self-concept.

There's no fixed script about what exactly to say when you talk to yourself, but speaking from the right frame of mind (i.e. from a position of self-respect and compassion) will get you most of the way. Nobody can tell you precisely the right words to use in your own mental dialogue. Your life context is unique, and every new situation will require you to respond spontaneously and authentically.

Using a pre-written script is a great first step—a little like mental training wheels as you find your confidence. But in time it should be easier to generate your own impromptu positive self-talk, in real time, and it will feel more and more genuine with practice. The end goal is not simply to rehearse a script, but to automatically and sincerely talk to yourself in a positive way.

Until that time, however, here's a brief self-talk checklist to make sure you're on the right track.

Positive self-talk should ideally be:

- Framed in present tense
- Simple and straightforward (statements that lead to endless cycles of rumination are likely to be negative self-talk whereas good, wholesome, affirmative self-talk is typically direct and uncomplicated)
- Honest, which means it must include potential room for improvement or shortcomings wherever relevant
- Personal and meaningful to you
- Able to make you feel better
- Practical and realistic
- Optimistic and hopeful—neutral is great, but if you're talking to yourself, why not be your own best friend and offer some supportive and encouraging words while you're at it?

Takeaways

- This chapter explores cognitive behavioral therapy (CBT) and other related techniques that can help us improve our self-talk. The whole aim of changing self-talk more or less falls under the process of CBT.
- CBT is a popular and effective therapeutic framework that emphasizes our thoughts as the key component of our feelings and behavior. The underlying principle of its techniques is that our thoughts influence how we feel, which in turn determines the way we behave. This creates a feedback loop that ultimately influences our thoughts, and the way to improve is to get out of this vicious cycle. We must replace our negative thoughts with more positive ones, with the condition that the latter be realistic and not merely vain self-affirmations that have no backing or truth to them. The general process for our purposes is to observe, challenge, and replace negative thoughts and self-talk.

- One effective method to reduce negative self-talk is an activity called thought stopping. This involves distracting yourself from troublesome thoughts using some behavioral or mental cues, such as thinking or saying "Stop!", pinching yourself, etc. Though this technique can backfire in some cases, it has been observed to be effective in curtailing superficial but unproductive rumination.
- Besides using cues, other ways to stop negative self-talk include listening to music or podcasts that you like. This distracts you by engaging your auditory faculties. You can also use scattered counting— counting random numbers instead of proceeding linearly like in 1,2,3, and so on. The idea is to catch yourself in the process and distance yourself from unhelpful thoughts.
- If thought stopping doesn't work, you can also practice thought replacing. Here, you take a negative thought and strip it of all the components that

make it unpleasant, replacing them with more positive alternatives. One way to do this is to simply think your thoughts through and assess how valid they are. If you find them to be irrational, substitute ones that make more sense to you and promote healthier emotions.

- Alternatively, you can write particular thoughts down to edit and rewrite them. Eliminate extreme words like only, never, absolutely, etc., along with any harsh descriptors like idiot, loser, ugly, and others. Also replace outright lies, unfounded assumptions, and other logical faults to improve your self-talk.

Chapter 5: More Than Words

Let's remind ourselves *why* we bothered to change our negative self-talk to healthier, more affirming self-talk.

The words inside our head are just words—but they have powerful, tangible effects on the world we live in because those words directly impact our behavior and the actions we take, every day. When these words are negative, they lead to anxiety, depression, self-pity, inaction, and all sorts of undesirable outcomes. However, when they're positive, they can carry you through even the darkest of times and help you emerge even stronger.

As you practice better awareness of your own self-talk and learn to rewrite the scripts that are holding you back, you will naturally start to notice that you may behave differently, make different choices, say different words out loud to others, and take different actions.

Self-talk is internal, but it's also the way we interface with our external reality. Bearing this in mind, our final chapter will focus on all the ways we can use external factors to support and encourage our positive self-talk. The relationship is reciprocal: good self-talk leads to healthy choices and behaviors, which themselves re-affirm good self-talk.

Our focus so far has been on the words we say quietly and internally to ourselves, but plenty of other elements affect our self-talk. The kinds of friends we have, the situations we put ourselves in, the media we expose ourselves to, our environment, our daily habits—all of these feed information into our self-talk engine and make it harder or easier to maintain self-esteem and compassion. While we can't control all these external factors, what we can control is how we perceive and respond to them and the influence they wield over us.

Everyday Reinforcement

Mindlessly saying a mantra into a mirror each morning when you don't really believe it is unlikely to have much effect. But by this point in the book, you've hopefully zoomed in on those alternative thoughts and core beliefs that directly challenge the negative self-talk that is unique to you and your life.

Starting each morning with a deliberately positive session of self-talk sets the tone and intention for the rest of the day. It's making a commitment to yourself to frame the rest of the day positively, with you set up as your own best friend and supporter.

The words you speak to yourself inside your head have a way of extending themselves outside your head and becoming real. You'll unconsciously use the same language out loud or when talking to others, which will in turn affect how they respond to you. Start the day on a life-affirming, hopeful footing and you'll not only find it's easier to be compassionate with yourself, but with others, too.

Negative thoughts lead to negative words and actions, and negativity toward other people that is likely to be reflected back to you. It seems like such a simple thing, but it makes all the difference in the world.

Do you begin your day with gratitude and optimism, speaking kindly to those around you and giving yourself the pep talk you need to get through the day's challenges? Or do you complain about everything that went wrong, assume the worst of those around you, find fault in everything and predict disaster at every turn?

It's all a choice. And good choices have a habit of breeding more good choices. This book is about the little words we say to ourselves in our minds, but it's about so much more than that—it's about our attitude to life itself, our entire mindset, our perspective on all our important relationships, and the engine that drives all the major decisions of our life.

So, a cheesy mantra said without conviction is not enough! That said, affirmations and positive scripts can be an immensely powerful way to retrain a mind stuck in negative self-talk. Our mind doesn't innately know right from wrong; it believes what we feed into it. That's why positive affirmations work. Use your words for good.

Regularly get some distance from yourself and your thoughts through meditation, journaling, or literally telling yourself "this is just a thought." Give your inner critic a name, so you can say, "Oh it's just Gertrude again, I can ignore her!" The important lesson here is that your thoughts aren't you, they're simply words that may or may not be true. Practice thought stopping or visualize putting useless self-talk in a box where it can't distract you. Then actively replace these thoughts with ones you've consciously chosen as supportive and more realistic—i.e. mantras, affirmations or scripts.

These can seem a little glib and silly on the surface, but they really work. It doesn't really help to just copy inspiring messages you hear from others, as nice as they may be. You need to choose words that personally resonate and speak directly to your unique core messages.

A good mantra can capture the essence of the attitude you want to emulate. Successful people often use mantras as positive personal mottos that they regularly rely on to boost their confidence and help them navigate adversity.

For example:

"You've survived worse before!" (Halts catastrophic thinking—you tell yourself that even the worst outcome is something you are strong enough to deal with.)

"You'll figure it out." (Shifts you into a more practical, objective frame of mind and away from rumination.)

"What matters most right now?" (Gets you out of obsessive thought loops and onto your values and goals.)

"I choose my own experience." (Empowers you to take charge of your ability to consciously rewrite your own script.)

"I am of value and I have purpose in this world." (Affirms that you are a human being with real worth who deserves care and respect, no matter what.)

"Will this matter in six months?" (Puts things in perspective!)

"The past is the past. What can I do now?" (Switches your focus to where it matters—action in the present moment.)

"There are always options." (Takes you out of black-and-white, doom-and-gloom thinking and into the realm of possibilities.)

"You're doing your best. Well done." (Self-affirmation that doesn't depend on outcome—acknowledges the hard work you're doing.)

"You rock!" (A little cheesy, but cuts to the chase—you have worth and are a valuable, lovable person. *No matter what.*)

"I'm unique in the world and nobody is like me." (Reminds you not to make comparisons.)

"Which path do you want to go down?" (We all have choices. This reminds you that you can always pour your energy and attention into what matters.)

"Today, I choose peace, gratitude and love, for myself and others." (Reasserts your values as an antidote to negativity, and asserts your power to control your own inner reality.)

"It's not how many times you fall down, it's how many times you get up." (Refocuses your attention on learning, and not getting bogged down in "failure.")

When something doesn't go right or you're struggling, pulling out a mantra or affirmation is like giving yourself a leg up, or having your own built-in guru who is on your side, cheering you on. It can definitely feel cheesy, but why not put some of these affirmations somewhere prominent where you can see them every day? Remember, the more something is repeated, the more your brain believes it's real.

A mantra or affirmation is a great way to cement positive self-talk and a healthy self-esteem, but there are other ways to support yourself, too. It would be a shame to nurture your self-esteem only to have it cancelled out by unsupportive or hostile people or situations around you.

As you practice affirming your own self-worth and working on your self-talk, you might more clearly notice the negative people in your life. You don't need to cut someone out of your life completely just because they had a bad day or ranted a little too much at your last meeting. Rather, it's about carefully noticing whether some people *consistently* affect your self-concept and self-talk in a negative way.

The attitudes of people around you can greatly influence your own. Though good friends support one another through challenges, pay attention if you have friends or family members who seem to steadily complain without taking any action, bring others down, are abusive, or simply have an air of negativity around them that makes everyone feel bad.

It can be hard to reduce your contact with such people, and it's not something to be done lightly. However, if you can see a regular and ongoing pattern of negativity that threatens your own efforts to maintain hope and optimism, it's time to set up a boundary. Limit time spent together or cut it out entirely, if possible. Your attitude to negative people who try to bring you down is not much different from your attitude to negative self-talk: recognize it for what it is and proactively move away from it.

Finally, keep a close eye on the media you consume. Do you spend ages online reading anxiety-inducing news articles? Do you waste hours on social media that only leaves you feeling worthless and out of the loop? Do you deliberately seek out information to confirm negative core beliefs?

Think of the media and the internet in general as a person—what kind of relationship do you have? It may be time to choose more balanced, healthy media to consume or step away from social media completely if you notice it eating away at your self-esteem. Can you find sources of information that inspire and encourage you rather than leave you feeling bad?

A Self-Empowerment Habit

The more you practice positive self-talk and cultivate a healthy self-esteem, the more and more your attitude will seep out into the world at large, affecting every part of your life. You may start to realize that healthy self-talk is just one small aspect of a healthy lifestyle; it's not just about supporting your mental health, but your entire well-being.

It's the little daily habits that accumulate and build a robust sense of confidence over time. It's the consistent effort and commitment to choosing the life you want that makes the difference. Self-talk is the ultimate habit in that it is something you're engaged with throughout the day, every day, for your entire life. But other habits can also weigh in on your overall self-concept and well-being.

Gratitude

The last thing your inner critic wants to do is appreciate the little things in life, or notice how lovely the sunset looks right now. Gratitude seems like a small thing, but it can be an incredibly powerful antidote to complaining, chronic anxiety, and dissatisfaction with the way things are—the essence of most negative self-talk.

The effects are backed up by science—a 2013 paper in *Psychology Today* showed that young people who kept gratitude journals experienced more energy, determination, attention, and feelings of enthusiasm than those who didn't. Gratitude changes the brain's focus, boosting serotonin and dopamine levels, and helping us feel more resilient in the face of challenges.

A gratitude journal is a place where you can consciously write down the things you are grateful for—a great cup of coffee in the morning, your pet doing something cute, sunshine on your skin, a beautiful song, a hug from a friend. Big or small, note it down so your brain has something tangible to focus on. Aim for three to five things a day—and you can always find a few things to be grateful for, no matter how tiny!

Closely related to this habit of gratitude is the habit of avoiding comparison. Like complaining, comparing yourself to others only robs your life of joy and keeps you focused on the negative. When you compare yourself to someone else, you deliberately ignore all the unique, wonderful things that make you *you*, while emphasizing perceived weakness and deficits that might not even be real.

Concentrating on what you don't have is a game that goes nowhere. You might see someone else's life and be envious of their financial situation, their relationships or families, their health and appearance, their talent and achievements, and so on.

But this is usually a distortion—you don't get to see inside that person's head to *their* self-talk, and you probably don't see their challenges, their fears, failures, shortcomings or anxieties. What others present to the world is typically the "highlights reel"—all the best parts of their lives.

What you don't see is what they're ashamed or unsure about; the hidden debt, the unhappy marriages, the mental health issues, and even the low self-esteem. You may be surprised to know that the person you admire and envy feels no better about themselves than you do, and actively wishes they were someone else!

Is there someone in the world who is objectively doing better than you? Of course. Does it matter? No.

There are also very many people doing worse, and when you think about it, how can you really measure this "better" or "worse" anyway? The truth is that everyone's life is very, very different, and most people are doing their very best with the gifts and limitations they have. Ultimately, someone else's life doesn't imply a single thing about you and your own life.

Try to adopt an attitude of compassion and kindness for everyone, even those annoying people who seem so perfect! Everyone is facing an uphill internal battle that we may not be aware of, and it's always advisable to be a positive influence on those around us. Practice taking joy in others' accomplishments, compliment them and be happy for them, knowing that it will never undermine your own value. They're not "better" than you, but they may well have knowledge, attributes and skills that you can learn from. Take inspiration from them and let them inspire you to work hard toward what you care about.

At the same time, understand that everybody is on a unique path. Comparison is not only unhelpful, it's also impossible. Life is not a race or a competition.

If you regularly find yourself comparing your life to others', ask what's really important, *to you*, and how you can bring those things to life. It's not your business what other people do, but it is your business what you do—focus as much as you can on your own self-determined values, goals and strengths, and you will never feel threatened by anyone else doing the same.

The Culmination of Rewriting Your Self-Talk

In this book, we've covered a number of different activities, approaches, techniques and methods to not only recognizing and understanding our self-talk, but actively rewriting the script and creating a better self-esteem. We've talked about the power of meditation, journaling, exercise, reframing and switching perspectives, thought-stopping techniques, relaxation methods, de-scripting and more.

But ultimately, all these activities point to one underlying aspect behind all these approaches: cultivating self-compassion.

What's the difference between someone who has naturally high self-esteem and who regularly engages in positive self-talk, and someone who doesn't? It's not that they've mastered any particular technique. Rather, *it's that they love and respect themselves, and conduct both their inner and outer worlds to reflect that deep belief.*

While the concept of high self-esteem was the focus of psychological research in the '80s and '90s, today more and more attention is being paid to self-compassion, and how it helps us reach our full potential beyond the old theories of high confidence. While the temporary boost that comes from comparing ourselves to others or putting others down can feel good, lasting feelings of self-worth derive from somewhere deeper.

In the past, parents were encouraged to tell their children they could be anything they wanted, and that they were special and different. But is that really true? And do we *need* to be special or different to deserve care, respect and consideration?

Praise and affirmation are great—but we need a sense of self that goes beyond this; we need to be able to remain solidly within our compassionate self-concept *despite* adversity, criticism, failure or weaknesses. Anyone can feel great when complimented, but do you have a sense of self strong enough to remain sure of your value even if nobody else sees it, and you aren't praised?

The solution is not to evaluate yourself and give yourself a high rating, *but not to evaluate yourself at all.* No labels. No judgment, good or bad.

Just acceptance of ourselves, exactly as we are, right now.

Many people unconsciously hold back on being kind to themselves, because they believe that they haven't earnt it, or that being too nice to themselves will make them lazy or selfish. Isn't that crazy, when you really stop to think about it?

What we could aim for is neither self-criticism ("you're hideous"), nor trying to prop ourselves up with false self-esteem ("you're way better looking than him"), but finding that calm, rational space in the middle where we love and accept however we are in this moment ("I look how I look. I accept that. I deserve love in any case").

Self-compassion is deeper and more lasting than high confidence because it is not dependent on fleeting external factors. If I attach my self-worth to being wealthy, or fit, or clever, it means my self-worth will disappear if I lose my money, fall ill or encounter someone more intelligent than I am. In other words, only internal, self-determined worth is true worth.

Self-compassion is not just something that sounds nice—it's backed up by solid research as a way to achieve greater well-being, contentment, emotional regulation (less anxiety and depression) and resilience. A 2008 paper by Neff and Vonk in the *Journal of Personality* showed that self-esteem and self-compassion are fundamentally different—and that self-compassion may surpass self-esteem in many ways. Perhaps best of all, being kind to ourselves makes it easier for us to be accepting of others, connecting mindfully with our common humanity.

Practice gentleness, understanding and kindness that doesn't depend on anything at all—simply give them to yourself and others for free, just like that. No ego needed. With self-compassion you don't take things personally, and seem to avoid some of the common pitfalls of overly high self-esteem—for example narcissism, feeling disappointed by neutral feedback, feeling like a failure because you're average, or having a sense of self that yoyos along with life's ups and downs.

Self-compassion says that *you are a human being and have intrinsic worth* that has nothing to do with who approves of you, your actions, failures, fears, or anything else. It's unconditional. This means you're OK with who you are, warts and all, and embrace even your imperfections, rather than claim there aren't any or work intently to get rid of them.

Self-compassion says, "Relax. Forget about asking whether you're good enough. You're alive and you're OK, exactly as you are." Open your heart, let things be as they are, and you'll find it much, much easier to drop the habit of beating yourself up.

An unexpected benefit of self-compassion is that it seems to remind us of a more universal sense of our interconnectivity, of our shared experience as human beings. It invites us to connect with something bigger than our tumultuous egos. With self-compassion, we paradoxically recognize the joy there is in serving others, and we develop a rich worldview that prioritizes the truly important things in life.

Actually being kind to yourself is harder than it seems at first—for some people, almost impossible. We might find that being hard on ourselves has been so effective at pushing us to do better that we're afraid to lose our motivation by allowing ourselves to relax. But there's a good way to bootstrap yourself into more self-compassion: imagine talking to yourself as you literally would to one of your dearest friends. This is because even those with the harshest self-talk can often summon up incredible depths of care and kindness for those they love— the trick is just to transfer it to themselves!

How do you treat a friend who is feeling down, scared, nervous, or who has just made a mistake? You probably don't tell them they're a complete idiot and that nobody loves them! So why do you do it to yourself?

The first thing to do is drop the idea that self-compassion means you're being indulgent. The truth is that kindness, understanding, and empathy almost certainly make you a better employee, spouse, friend, and person in general. Once you realize that your inner critic isn't actually making you a better person but instead undermining you, you are free to give yourself the support that will actually improve your life.

Imagine a toddler who bursts into tears because they are frustrated they can't tie their shoelaces. You wouldn't laugh at them, tell them they were useless or get angry that they were unhappy. You'd be patient, explain that they'd learn eventually, and that you still loved them no matter what. Do the same for yourself, especially when *you're* in the middle of a tantrum and feel like you're failing!

Use this approach every time you hear the voice of judgment and criticism emerging within you. Don't berate yourself for oversleeping; instead notice that you're not getting enough rest and choose to care enough about yourself to go to bed earlier that night.

Don't agree with the rude person who insulted you on the bus—put a boundary up and tell yourself, "It's them, not me," then forget about it. Don't psyche yourself out with self-doubt as you write your resume, but look over your own shoulder and give yourself some encouragement: "I know this is hard but you're great. You're doing good work."

When negative thoughts pop up, recognize that it's just the inner critic speaking, like a monster under the bed. If it has something useful to say, listen, but don't entertain any idea that damages your well-being or isn't true. Would you allow a random stranger to waltz up to a loved one on the street and tell them, "You're worthless, and you don't deserve to be here"? Have the same reaction for yourself—even if you're the one who's being mean to you!

A great exercise is to write out a "job description" for your inner critic. What is their main function in your life, really, and how do they go about doing that work? Do you let them? Is your inner critic keeping you safe or are they limiting you? Are they supporting you or breaking you down? What effect do they have on your life? Are their words motivational or do they do the opposite of inspire?

Looking at your inner critic as a separate entity who is only doing their job gives you some distance and perspective on negative self-talk when it appears. How will you play manager to this employee? Just like it's a mosquito's job to occasionally bite you, you will sometimes encounter negativity in your life. But that doesn't mean you have to accept it!

Takeaways

- Previously we discussed how to rewrite our internal monologue, but in this chapter we focused on all the external factors that contribute to having healthier and more positive self-talk. There are everyday practices we can do to contribute to a more positive self-image, or just snap us into sharper awareness of our beliefs and narratives.

- Starting your morning with a dose of deliberately positive self-talk sets a pleasant tone for the rest of your day. While it may feel silly to feign positivity in the beginning, this technique really does work. The more we repeat something to ourselves, the likelier we are to start believing it (remember neuroplasticity?). By repeating positive statements that represent our desired goals throughout the day, we can easily boost our confidence and self-esteem in the face of adversity.
- Having said that, we are bound to struggle in remaining positive if those around us continue to be negative and judgmental. As we practice positive self-talk, we're more likely to notice the negativities of our friends and families. In such cases, we must set good boundaries to limit

our interactions with negative people in our lives, and even refrain from it altogether if required.

- Many of our habits, when cultivated properly, can help reinforce positive self-talk in our lives. For example, learning to be grateful is a great way to increase our overall happiness. Maintain a gratitude journal and update it daily with three to five things you were grateful for on that day as a way to count your blessings. Other productive habits include avoiding comparisons with others, being kind in your interactions, and avoiding overly critical thought patterns.

- Another healthy habit we must develop is practicing self-compassion. This merely involves treating ourselves with more kindness and generosity. Too often, we are our own worst critics, but being compassionate to yourself is a tried and tested method for improving your self-esteem, happiness, and overall health. One easy way to do this is to talk to yourself as you would to a dear friend. We are generally much more accepting of our friends' mistakes than our own, and we must extend the same courtesy to ourselves.

Summary Guide

Chapter 1. That Voice Inside Your Head

- Have you ever noticed a voice inside your head that is constantly chattering about something or the other right from the moment you wake up? You might have grown so accustomed to it that you barely notice it anymore, but it's definitely there, and it's either hurting or helping you. No perspective is truly neutral. This voice, a part of your stream of consciousness, is an inner monologue that runs alongside your life, observing and commenting on its various happenings. It tells you who you are, and how you should feel about your identity and the events that occur in your life.
- There are three main types of inner voices or self-talk. The first is positive self-talk, which acts as a

continuous reaffirmation of the good things about you and your life. This type of inner voice bolsters our confidence and elevates happiness levels. However, on the other end lies negative self-talk. This voice is always critical and saying degrading things to us about who we are, what we do, etc. If left uncontrolled, it can lead to several mental health issues. The third type is neutral self-talk, which simply consists of unbiased observations as we walk through life—although this almost always has a positive or negative subtext.

- Our inner voice, regardless of type, represents the inner representation we have of ourselves. Often, this is not consistent with reality. The way we think we are and what we actually are can be miles apart, but reality seldom matters if we're convinced that things are a certain way. This leads to why having healthy self-talk is so important. It influences our thoughts, perceptions, and the way we view ourselves, all of

which have physiological correlations that affect how we feel and behave. The basis behind this is neuroplasticity, as the more you repeat something, the more it changes your brain's structure and becomes your reality.
- If you're wondering what exactly counts as self-talk, it includes positive or negative statements we say to ourselves, our ruminations, racing thoughts, and the conversations we have with ourselves. Regulating this self-talk can have many positive effects that are essential to our well-being, such as improving sports performances, reducing stress, promoting better self-esteem, and helping us cope with the ups and downs of life. Monitoring self-talk is the key to changing your emotions, behavior, perspective, and life potential.

Chapter 2. Good Versus Evil

- It is easy to mistake positive self-talk for being vain, narcissistic, and shallow, overloading oneself with praise—but this is far from the case. Similarly, ignoring negative self-talk does not mean blinding yourself to your faults. Improving our self-talk is aimed at being more attuned with reality in a way that is conducive to achieving the goals we desire. Often we focus on the negative much more than the positive, and this distorts the reality of a situation. By practicing more positive self-talk, we're trying to get past this bias and see things the way they are so that we can improve accordingly.
- There are many benefits of engaging in more positive self-talk. Several studies have looked into the matter and concluded that those who are more positive perform better at work and sports, are better at getting through challenging life circumstances, and have healthier relationships. Moreover, they also have a better self-image and feel

good about themselves since they have a healthy sense of self.
- On the other hand, negative self-talk can be extremely damaging to our well-being. It releases cortisol in our bodies, compromising our immune function and preventing positive emotions from arising. Negative self-talk can also lead to a host of mental health issues such as depression, anxiety, panic disorders, and other undesirable outcomes like apathy, anger, self-pity, etc.
- If you're wondering where our self-talk styles originate from, the answer is a host of factors that include our parenting, socio-cultural norms, our immediate environment, biology, our own biases and beliefs, among others. Many who have experienced strict or uncompromising home environments at a young age, or have routinely had their boundaries violated, come to adopt a low self-esteem, which in turn causes negative self-talk that can be hard to get rid of.

- These factors, along with experiences like bullying and different forms of abuse, also determine our self-esteem levels, which is the main determinant of whether our self-talk is negative or positive. As we understand why exactly our self-talk is the way it is, we can start to change and improve it to suit our needs.

- We end up with five levels of self-talk, each a higher amount of acceptance and self-esteem. Indeed, it starts with purely negative, then moves to aspirational, to positive, to a new identity, to newfound acceptance of both the negative and positive.

Chapter 3. All You Need to Do Is Listen

- The first step to recognizing and correcting your inner voice is to become aware of it. A powerful way to do this is through practicing mindfulness. Mindfulness is the

activity wherein you train your mind to become aware of your present emotions, sensations, or experience and accept them without clouding them with any judgment.
- There are many different mindfulness activities you can follow. One of them is called the three-minute breathing space and it proceeds in three steps, as follows. First, simply take in all your thoughts and observe them without attempting to control their flow. Then, narrow your focus away from them and simply concentrate on your breathing for a minute. Lastly, expand your focus to include your body and physical sensations. Activities like these help you recognize your thoughts and move on from them without overthinking.
- As you practice mindfulness, you will become aware of some negative thinking patterns that we commonly engage in. One of them is called black and white thinking, where we mislead ourselves into looking at the

world in strictly binary terms. Another is catastrophizing, which involves drawing exaggerated conclusions from comparatively minor incidents. Patterns like these distort our thinking and obscure the nature of reality.

- Journaling is a powerful tool for not only recognizing negative thought patterns, but also challenging them to come up with more rational and thought-out alternatives. Writing your thoughts makes them seem more tangible, and allows you to evaluate them better than when it's all in your head.
- However, if journaling doesn't sound suitable to you, there are other ways to assess your self-talk. Reflect on your negative thoughts and core beliefs as they come to you and compassionately, but systematically challenge them. Play the role of a lawyer and look for logical holes. Try to identify the thinking patterns that are distorting your self-talk, and

work on replacing them with healthier thoughts.

Chapter 4. Replace, Transform, Evolve

- This chapter explores cognitive behavioral therapy (CBT) and other related techniques that can help us improve our self-talk. The whole aim of changing self-talk more or less falls under the process of CBT.
- CBT is a popular and effective therapeutic framework that emphasizes our thoughts as the key component of our feelings and behavior. The underlying principle of its techniques is that our thoughts influence how we feel, which in turn determines the way we behave. This creates a feedback loop that ultimately influences our thoughts, and the way to improve is to get out of this vicious cycle. We must replace our negative thoughts with more positive ones, with the condition that the latter be realistic and not merely

vain self-affirmations that have no backing or truth to them. The general process for our purposes is to observe, challenge, and replace negative thoughts and self-talk.
- One effective method to reduce negative self-talk is an activity called thought stopping. This involves distracting yourself from troublesome thoughts using some behavioral or mental cues, such as thinking or saying "Stop!", pinching yourself, etc. Though this technique can backfire in some cases, it has been observed to be effective in curtailing superficial but unproductive rumination.
- Besides using cues, other ways to stop negative self-talk include listening to music or podcasts that you like. This distracts you by engaging your auditory faculties. You can also use scattered counting—counting random numbers instead of proceeding linearly like in 1,2,3, and so on. The idea is to catch yourself in

the process and distance yourself from unhelpful thoughts.
- If thought stopping doesn't work, you can also practice thought replacing. Here, you take a negative thought and strip it of all the components that make it unpleasant, replacing them with more positive alternatives. One way to do this is to simply think your thoughts through and assess how valid they are. If you find them to be irrational, substitute ones that make more sense to you and promote healthier emotions.

- Alternatively, you can write particular thoughts down to edit and rewrite them. Eliminate extreme words like only, never, absolutely, etc., along with any harsh descriptors like idiot, loser, ugly, and others. Also replace outright lies, unfounded assumptions, and other logical faults to improve your self-talk.

Chapter 5: More Than Words

- Previously we discussed how to rewrite our internal monologue, but in this chapter we focused on all the external factors that contribute to having healthier and more positive self-talk. There are everyday practices we can do to contribute to a more positive self-image, or just snap us into sharper awareness of our beliefs and narratives.
- Starting your morning with a dose of deliberately positive self-talk sets a pleasant tone for the rest of your day. While it may feel silly to feign positivity in the beginning, this technique really does work. The more we repeat something to ourselves, the likelier we are to start believing it (remember neuroplasticity?). By repeating positive statements that represent our desired goals throughout the day, we can easily boost our confidence and self-esteem in the face of adversity.
- Having said that, we are bound to struggle in remaining positive if

those around us continue to be negative and judgmental. As we practice positive self-talk, we're more likely to notice the negativities of our friends and families. In such cases, we must set good boundaries to limit our interactions with negative people in our lives, and even refrain from it altogether if required.
- Many of our habits, when cultivated properly, can help reinforce positive self-talk in our lives. For example, learning to be grateful is a great way to increase our overall happiness. Maintain a gratitude journal and update it daily with three to five things you were grateful for on that day as a way to count your blessings. Other productive habits include avoiding comparisons with others, being kind in your interactions, and avoiding overly critical thought patterns.

- Another healthy habit we must develop is practicing self-compassion. This merely involves treating ourselves with more kindness and generosity. Too often, we are our own worst critics, but being compassionate to yourself is a tried and tested method for improving your self-esteem, happiness, and overall health. One easy way to do this is to talk to yourself as you would to a dear friend. We are generally much more accepting of our friends' mistakes than our own, and we must extend the same courtesy to ourselves.

www.ingramcontent.com/pod-product-compliance
Lightning Source LLC
Chambersburg PA
CBHW071345080526
44587CB00017B/2973